List camping gear
Jumper Cables

An Introduction to Computer Hardware

WINTHROP COMPUTER SYSTEMS SERIES

Gerald M. Weinberg, editor

COATS AND PARKIN

Computer Models in the Social Sciences

CONWAY AND GRIES

Primer on Structured Programming Using PL/I, PL/C, and PL/CT

CONWAY, GRIES, AND WORTMAN

Introduction to Structured Programming Using PL/I and SP/k

CONWAY, GRIES, AND ZIMMERMAN

A Primer on PASCAL

CONWAY

A Primer on Disciplined Programming Using PL/I, PL/CS, and PL/CT

CRIPPS

An Introduction to Computer Hardware

EASLEY

Primer for Small Systems Management

FINKENAUR

COBOL for Students: A Programming Primer

GELLER AND FREEDMAN

Structured Programming in APL

GILB

Software Metrics

GILB AND WEINBERG

Humanized Input: Techniques for Reliable Keyed Input

WEINBERG, WRIGHT, GOETZ, AND KAUFFMAN

High Level COBOL Programming

FUTURE TITLES

ECKHOUSE AND SPIER

Guide to Programming

GREENFIELD

The Architecture of Microcomputers

HEBDITCH

The Minicomputer in Terminal-Based Systems

LINES

Minicomputer Systems

POOCH

Simulation

SHNEIDERMAN

Human Factors in Computer and Information Systems

TOPPING

Simula Programming

WILCOX

Introduction to Compiler Construction

An Introduction to Computer Hardware

Martin Cripps

Department of Computing and Control
Imperial College of Science and Technology

Winthrop Publishers, Inc.
Cambridge, Massachusetts

Library of Congress Cataloging in Publication Data

Cripps,   Martin.
        An   introduction   to   computer   hardware.

        Includes index.
        1.   Computers.   I.   Title.
TK7885.C74   1978   621.3819'53   78-8549
ISBN   0-87626-396-1

For Margot and Norman

Published by
Edward Arnold (Publishers) Ltd.,
25 Hill Street, London W1X 8LL

Published in the U.S. by
Winthrop Publishers, Inc.
17 Dunster Street
Cambridge, Massachusetts 02138

Contents

5 Central Control Unit

6 Simple Input Output and Peripherals

7 Complex Input Output

8 Storage Media

9 Storage Arrangements

10 Computers, Communication and Reliability

11 Construction and Implementation

Preface

Computing is one of the most important - some might say the most
important - branches of science and technology. In reality it is
a technology and a servant to all sciences and technologies, for
it is useless to have a theory of computing unless there is
something useful to compute and machinery on which to perform the
computation.

This is an introductory book on the important topic of computer
hardware. It is vital for all users and programmers of computers
to appreciate the capabilities and restrictions of the machine
which will execute their programs. The basic technique of modern
computing is systems engineering, that is the software and
hardware are engineered into a total system. A computing
scientist or programmer requires a thorough understanding of
computer hardware if he is to make the best use of it. The aim of
this text is to present the material necessary for a good
understanding of the design, construction and operation of
computer hardware in a straightforward and logical fashion.

There are some excellent works on the detailed design and
hardware of computers for those with a good technological or
electronics background. However, students commence the study of
computing at school, as undergraduates at university or sometimes
as graduates in other subjects taking "conversion" courses. Their
background frequently contains no more than O-level or A-level
physics and little engineering or technology. This book was
produced in the absence of any cheap, well-structured texts and
was based on the notes produced for the undergraduate and
postgraduate courses which I developed and presented at Imperial
College. The book should also prove useful to anyone else not
directly studying computing, who wishes to remove any gulf
seperating him or her from the mystique of the "pretty coloured
boxes with the flashing lights".

Computing, in modern terms, is thirty years old this year,
although most of the ideas were foreshadowed by Charles Babbage
and Ada Augusta, Countess of Lovelace, between 1833 and Babbage's
death in 1871. In 1833 Babbage conceived the idea of his
"analytical engine", which was to include stored programs, a

store, an arithmetic unit which he called the "mill" and
input-output mechanisms. To be constructed using steel gears and
to be powered by steam, it was a conception far beyond the
technology of the time and was never finished. However, from
Babbage's drawings and the detailed descriptions and suggestions
for usage by his colleague the Countess of Lovelace, it is
apparent that their ideas were both brilliant and correct. Their
foresight even went as far as to point out that the analytical
engine (like all subsequent computers) "has no pretensions
whatever to originate anything".

A computer can do whatever we know how to order it to perform,
and nothing further. This is a point which all should hold firmly
in mind when discussing computers.

My approach is to divide the computer into logically separate
parts and to study them individually before putting them together
to create a complete machine. An introduction to the description
of logic and design precedes the main body of text. A description
of the technology used to implement the designs ends the book.

The assistance of Elsbeth Lindner who read the text and
suggested valuable improvements is gratefully acknowledged. The
comments, mostly polite and helpful, from students who have
attended my courses have contributed to the accuracy and
suitability of the text and are also much appreciated.

Martin Cripps,
London,
January 1977.

An Introduction to Computer Hardware

1 Basic Concepts

1.1   THE STORED PROGRAM MACHINE

The basic cycle of any computer is to *FETCH* instructions from a
store and then to *EXECUTE* them. The instructions must be fetched
in a predetermined sequence, so that they cause execution of the
actions the user requires to solve his problem. They must contain
sufficient information to determine these actions completely.
Instructions need to contain some, or all, of the information in
the form:

RESULT = OPERAND {OPERATOR} OPERAND   {NEXT INSTRUCTION}
E.G.   A=B+C, next instruction is at X.

No more information is ever required than these five "fields",
though that information may have to be found by means of pointers
to, or "addresses" in the store. It is usual for some of the
fields to be implicit in the design of the machine, for instance,
it is normal to assume that the next instruction is held in the
store location immediately following that of the instruction
being executed. Hence the next instruction field is implicit and
only when a change to the sequential fetching of instructions is
required is any information needed to tell the hardware (the
electronics) to get the next instruction from a location other
than the implied one.

The instruction to be performed, specified by the operator,
sets the machine to add, multiply, compare, etc, the operands
specified, and produce a result, which can then become an input
operand for some later instruction. The most important feature of
a computer is its ability to choose one of a number of different
sequences of instructions, depending on results it has calculated
previously.

To function in this way, a computer requires the following: a
store to hold the instructions and any data or operands; a
processing unit, often called an arithmetic and logic unit, to
perform the operations such as adding or comparing; a control
unit to ensure instructions and data are obtained from the store
correctly, and that the proper sequences are maintained; and a
set of input-output peripherals to communicate with the machine.

2 Basic Concepts

Computer hardware is essentially very simple. All the storage, control and processing elements can be constructed using a single electronic circuit containing only a few transistors, whereas a colour television requires many different circuits, using all kinds of components. With computers, the complexity comes not in the electronics or the circuits but in the way they are connected together. Fig.1.1 shows the connection of the five key elements described above and treated as "black boxes". This is the traditional way to view a computer. Each "box" can be looked at more or less independently and this will be done after a review of the basic circuits and the way they can be connected to give more complex units.

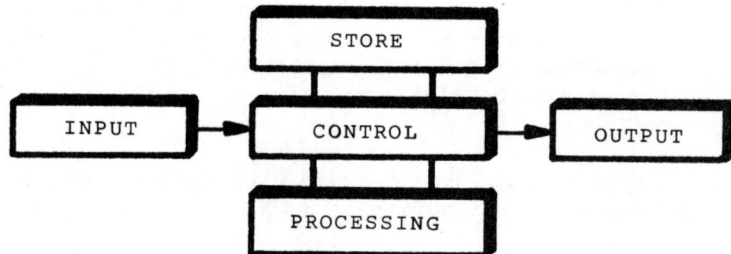

FIG. 1.1 A SIMPLE COMPUTER STRUCTURE

1.2 LOGIC CONVENTIONS

Signals which can take an infinite number of values or states are called analog signals and can be used, but as most computers use signals which can only have defined values or states, digital signals, these are used throughout this book. However, it should be borne in mind that both analog and hybrid computers are constructed as well as digital computers.

In most systems which process information in digital form, the signals are nominally two-valued or "binary" in nature. For example, information may be represented by a voltage or current which takes one of two values on a wire, or by a pulse of defined shape, which is either present or absent at a given time. In computers the two binary states are represented in different ways in different parts of the machine because of the physical nature of the devices which make up the machine. For a first discussion of computer logic it will be assumed that the states are defined by bands of voltage, with a forbidden region between them. Each band will be referred to by its nominal value, as in Fig.1.2

The more positive state has been arbitrarily chosen to represent the "1" or *TRUE* state: this is termed "positive" logic. The case where the "0" or *FALSE* state is the more positive and the true state more negative is called "negative" logic: the significance of this convention will become apparent further on. Also one of the levels has been chosen to be zero volts, which is obviously convenient as a switch being off gives zero volts and on, connected to a power supply, can give a positive voltage for the other state. If neither voltage is chosen to be zero volts, then the logic is called "bipolar". This is used for data communication, by the Post Office and others, as the "0" and "1" states are represented by voltages which are different from a failed state, such as a broken wire.

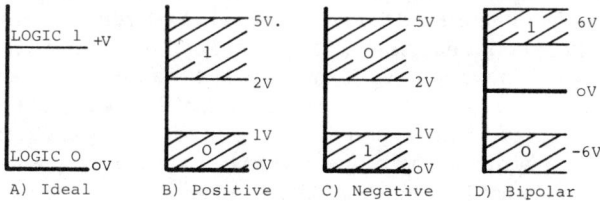

FIG. 1.2 LOGIC LEVELS AND NOMINAL VALUES

With the chosen definitions, switching arrangements could be devised, using relays or other types of switches, or using transistors in integrated circuits as in modern computers. It would obviously be inefficient to carry drawings of relays or transistor switch circuits through the whole design process, so logic "symbols" and "truth tables" are introduced to simplify drawing and to permit easy description of logic.

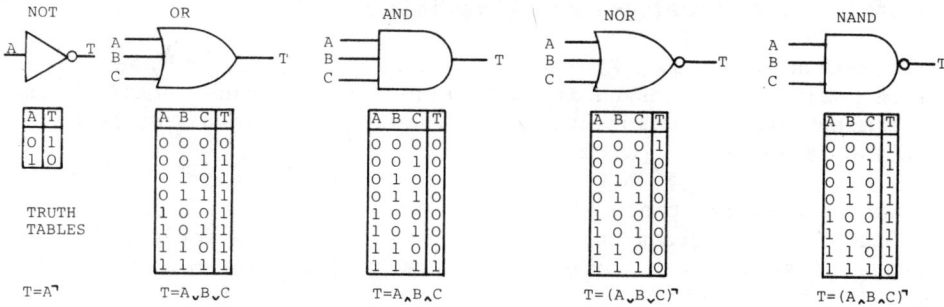

FIG. 1.3 SIMPLE LOGICAL ELEMENTS

The logical symbols, truth tables and Boolean expressions for all the simple logical elements are shown in Fig.1.3. The truth tables show the outputs which are produced for all possible different input combinations; the expressions are an algebraic description and are described later. The three basic elements are the inverter or NOT, the OR and the AND gates. The NOR and NAND gates, which are most common in computers because they happen to be easier to construct, are formed from OR and AND with an inverter following. As can be seen, an AND gate only produces a true output if *ALL* its inputs are true, so one input effectively acts as a gate to any others, shutting them off if it is false. An OR gate, on the other hand, acts as a union, combining inputs together, so that, if *ANY* input is true, the output is true.

The effect of positive and negative logic can now be seen. If the logic convention is changed, everything which represents "true" would represent "false" and vice versa. The physical circuit, which produced the NAND, would then produce a NOR, as can be shown by changing all 0's for 1's, and vice versa, in the truth tables. It is apparent that a single logic element, say a four input positive NAND, can also be made to perform as a NOR, by changing convention (to negative), and also as a NOT, by connecting all four inputs together (see the truth table). Even though a given design or logic diagram may call for a variety of gates, all the five basic ones can be "made" from just one. Storage elements can also be made from NAND and NOR gates.

1.3 BOOLEAN ALGEBRA, DEFINITIONS AND POSTULATES

Starting with the logical building blocks, complex logical functions could be designed by inspired guesswork, or experience, or a combination of both. This would not be very satisfactory, as there would be no checks on correctness of design, or on optimality in the design procedure. By using the logic of two-valued functions developed by the mathematician George Boole, we can produce formal design and optimisation techniques.

A Boolean variable "X" has two possible values, "0" and "1". These values are mutually exclusive. A Boolean function is determined when a relationship between two or more independant Boolean variables is given.

The following postulates (and notation) are adopted for addition, multiplication, inversion (complementation) and the logical functions in Boolean arithmetic and algebra. Each can occur in two forms, the second being the dual of the first. The dual of OR is AND and the dual of a variable is its complement.

INVERT	AND	OR	ADD	MULTIPLY
$\neg 0 = 1$	$0 \wedge 0 = 0$	$0 \vee 0 = 0$	$0+0 = 0$	$0.0 = 0$
$0^{\neg} = 1$	$0 \wedge 1 = 0$	$0 \vee 1 = 1$	$0+1 = 1$	$0.1 = 0$
$\neg 1 = 0$	$1 \wedge 0 = 0$	$1 \vee 0 = 1$	$1+0 = 1$	$1.0 = 0$
$1^{\neg} = 0$	$1 \wedge 1 = 1$	$1 \vee 1 = 1$	$1+1 = 0*$	$1.1 = 1$

*with a carry to the next bit.

1.4 ALGEBRAIC PROPERTIES AND BOOLEAN THEOREMS

Bearing in mind that Boolean variables can only take one of two possible values, the following algebraic properties of normal algebra also apply to Boolean algebra. Commutation implies that the order or sequence of variables has no effect on the value of an expression. Association implies that in sequences of only AND or of only OR functions, the placing of the parenthesis does not affect the result. The distributive property implies that an expression containing both AND and OR functions may be AND'ed out (multiplied out) with the AND taking precedence in a similar fashion to multiplication and addition in ordinary algebra.

COMMUTATIVE	$X_\wedge Y = Y_\wedge X$	$X_\vee Y = Y_\vee X$
ASSOCIATIVE	$X_\wedge(Y_\wedge Z) = (X_\wedge Y)_\wedge Z$	$X_\vee(Y_\vee Z) = (X_\vee Y)_\vee Z$
DISTRIBUTIVE	$X_\vee Y_\wedge Z = (X_\vee Y)_\wedge(X_\vee Z)$	$X_\wedge(Y_\vee Z) = (X_\wedge Y)_\vee(X_\wedge Z)$

The following provable theorems demonstrate the results of the logical functions on variables combined with a fixed "true" or "false", or with themselves or their complements. They can all be demonstrated by constructing the truth table, taking all possible combinations of true and false inputs and producing the output.

UNIT AND ZERO	$0_\vee X = X$	$1_\vee X = 1$	$0_\wedge X = 0$	$1_\wedge X = X$
IDEMPOTENCE	$X_\vee X = X$		$X_\wedge X = X$	
COMPLEMENTARITY	$X_\vee X^\neg = 1$		$X_\wedge X^\neg = 0$	
INVOLUTION	$(X^\neg)^\neg = X$			

The absorption theorem shows how commonly-occurring patterns of variables are reduced to simpler forms by removing the redundancies occurring in the theorems above.

ABSORPTION	$X_\vee X_\wedge Y = X$	$X_\wedge X_\vee Y = X$
	$X_\vee X^\neg{}_\wedge Y = X_\vee Y$	$X_\wedge X^\neg{}_\vee Y = X_\wedge Y$

The exchange of the logical operators OR and AND is arranged by using De Morgan's theorem. It is easily shown to be the same as the convention change between positive and negative logic discussed earlier. By changing all true and false variables to their complements, the operator required is also changed to its *DUAL* (AND to OR, NAND to NOR and vice versa).

DE MORGAN	$\neg(X_\vee Y) = \neg X_\wedge \neg Y \quad \neg(X_\wedge Y) = \neg X_\vee \neg Y$

The absorption theorem and De Morgan's theorem are the basis for all minimisation techniques, the aim of which are to remove any redundancy from Boolean expressions. This is desirable, as each redundant AND or OR implies a redundant gate, hence some redundant components, and so more optimal solutions would result from the formal application of these theorems. Logical units of considerable complexity can be constructed using the basic logical functions and these complex units can then be used as "black boxes" for further design stages. To formalise the design techniques, all types of logic need to be considered. There are three types, namely combinational, synchronous sequential and asynchronous sequential, and they are diagrammatically represented in Fig.1.4. Combinational logic contains no storage, so the outputs at any time are only dependant on the inputs. There is no effect due to "history", as there is with sequential logic, which contains storage, so that the outputs depend on the inputs and on previous states which have been held. The difference between synchronous and asynchronous logic is that, whilst in the former a clock is used and changes are only acted on at predetermined times, so that stored states only alter at fixed times, in the latter changes can occur at any time and states may change at any time. Asynchronous sequential logic can give rise to "races" where two signals change and the order in which they change may not always be the same.

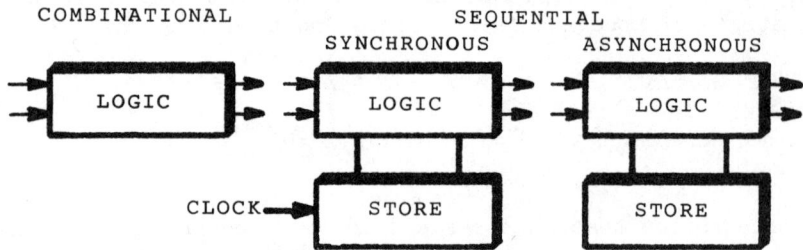

FIG. 1.4 *LOGIC CIRCUIT FORMS*

There are formal design techniques for all 3 types of logic, but the sequential logic design methods are complicated, seldom performed by hand and are well described in books on logic design. A simple example of one formal technique for combinational logic design is described to demonstrate the approach to such problems.

Starting from the truth table, various forms of Boolean expression can be produced, some of which are very useful, particularly the "canonical" or standard form.

If all elementary elements or their complements occur once only in each factor, then the expression is in canonical form. If the expression is in the form: $\{A \wedge B \wedge \neg C\} \vee \{\neg A \wedge B \wedge C\} \vee \{A \wedge \neg B \wedge C\}$, then it is in the *MINTERM* (or sum of products form), and if it is in the form: $\{A \vee \neg B \vee C\} \wedge \{\neg A \vee B \vee \neg C\}$, then it is in the *MAXTERM* (or product of sums form). Both these expressions are also canonical, whereas $\{A \wedge B\} \vee \{A \wedge \neg B \wedge C\} \vee \{\neg C \wedge D\}$ is a minterm form but not canonical.

1.5 KARNAUGH MAP DESIGN (K-MAP)

A K-map is the most common simple minimisation technique and is based on the layout of combinations of elementary variables such that only one elementary variable changes between adjacent squares on the map. This change corresponds to the $X \lor X^{\neg}=1$ function, so the variable may be removed without affecting the final function. As can be seen in Fig.1.5, the value of the squares 0,1,2 (equivalent to binary 000, 001, 010, etc.) is the value of a term of the canonical minterm form, hence its importance. This coding scheme which changes in one bit only is called the "Gray code".

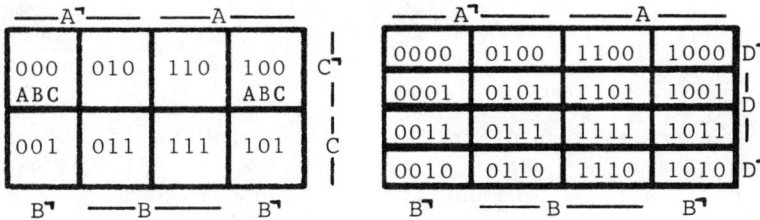

FIG. 1.5 THREE AND FOUR VARIABLE K MAPS

EXAMPLE: The truth table for a function is shown in Fig.1.6. The expression can be read off directly by an OR function between all the AND combinations, which are to provide a true (1) output. Alternatively, if there are fewer false indications than true required for output, then the method can be applied to them if an inversion is added, as the answer generated will be NOT what is required. The expression can be plotted onto a K-map directly and reduction is performed by combining adjacent squares into the fewest number of larger squares or rectangles. Each time two adjacent squares contain a 1, the function $X \lor X^{\neg}=1$ must occur, so the common variable is redundant at that point.

$$T = A^{\neg}_\land B_\land C \lor A_\land B^{\neg}_\land C \lor A_\land B_\land C^{\neg} \lor A_\land B_\land C = A_\land B \lor B_\land C \lor C_\land A \text{ (reduced)}$$

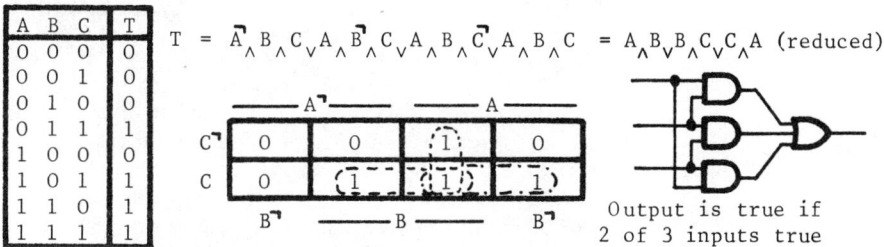

FIG. 1.6 EXAMPLE OF K MAP DESIGN

If a NAND only form is required, it can be obtained by applying De Morgan's theorem, as in the example, giving a NAND:NAND implementation instead of the NOT:AND:OR form. K-maps close on their edges, i.e. square 1000 is also adjacent to squares 0000, 1010. This technique can be used for up to 6 variables by hand; thereafter a computer is used. The better computer minimisation techniques are tabular and will handle any number of variables, the best known being the Quinne-McCluskey technique, which is well described in the literature. When plotting onto a K-map, it can be useful to use any outputs where you "do not care" whether the output is 1 or 0. They are plotted as # on the map and can be used, or not, at will.

So far only combinational logic has been described, where no previous states are relevant, but for a computer, storage will be required, as will circuits which can react depending on some past state or event.

1.6 BISTABLE CIRCUITS

Bistable circuits can exist indefinitely in one of two stable, separate states. By connecting two NOR gates with feedback, as shown in fig.1.7, an element which depends on previous inputs as well as current inputs can be made. It will store one state or binary digit, often called a *BIT*, and is sometimes called a staticisor or a "flipflop". The Boolean expression for the circuit is: $Q = \neg\{R \vee \neg\{Q \vee S\}\}$ and the truth table shows how it reacts, depending on its previous state (P=previous state, Q=current state).

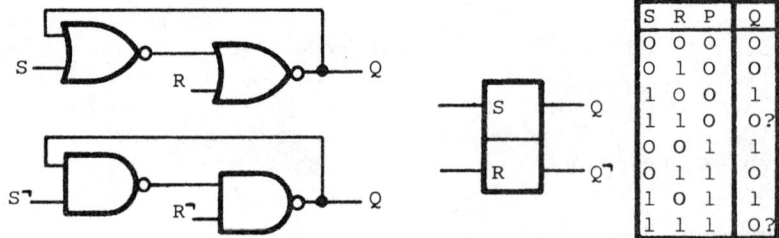

S	R	P	Q
0	0	0	0
0	1	0	0
1	0	0	1
1	1	0	0?
0	0	1	1
0	1	1	0
1	0	1	1
1	1	1	0?

FIG. 1.7 THE SET RESET {SR} BISTABLE

This "SR" bistable has one major drawback, which occurs when S=R=1. The final output Q, when S and R are both removed, is not determined. One can design so that this combination never occurs, but it is easier to have an element without this drawback. If only data is to be stored and the element is not required to be able to be set and reset independantly, then a "D-type" bistable is used. This has a single data input which is latched by a short clock pulse.

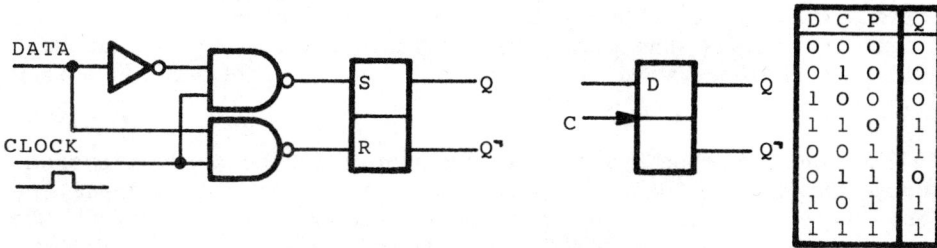

D	C	P	Q
0	0	0	0
0	1	0	0
1	0	0	0
1	1	0	1
0	0	1	1
0	1	1	0
1	0	1	1
1	1	1	1

FIG. 1.8 THE D TYPE BISTABLE

The D-type responds to a data input by retaining its value when the control line (or clock line) makes the transition from true to false. It responds on an "edge" and the circuit is shown with the truth table in Fig.1.8. This element is used to build data registers which hold many binary digits in parallel and hence a complete number.

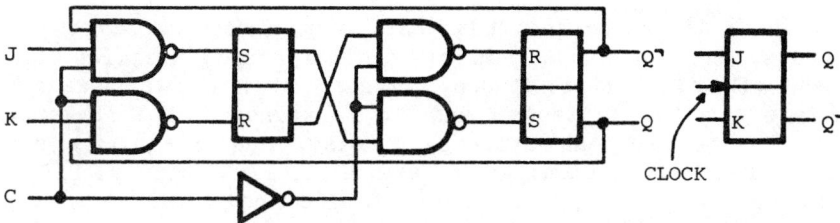

FIG. 1.9 THE JK BISTABLE

The "JK" or master-slave bistable is the one used most frequently when independent set and reset conditions are required. For instance, if a printer is to start on a given set of conditions and end on a different set, the JK of Fig.1.9 would be used to control it. The truth table for the JK is the same as for the RS except for the two undetermined states, which are arranged so that the output changes if the J and K inputs are both "1". Another useful property of the JK is that the output appears only when the clock is removed, so the JK acts as a delay of 1 clock pulse. It contains an RS within it, if one wants to use one in a design predominantly using JK's.

1.7 REGISTERS

A single state can be retained over time in a bistable, hence storing a group of bits in a parallel set of bistables, or register, as in Fig.1.10, will permit a number to be stored. Number representation is covered in more detail in Chapter 2, but as well as numbers, logical values, true or false, sometimes referred to as *FLAGS*, and characters will be needed. A single flag requires a single bit, but they are normally grouped together to give the same length *WORD* as for numbers. In most minicomputers the word length is 16 bits, as this is convenient for instructions, numbers and characters.

The normal number system used by people is the decimal system, using the digits 0-9 and columns for units, tens and hundreds. We are able to use other systems easily, for example the "duodecimal" (12) system for feet and inches, where columns represent twelves and "hundred and fourty-fours". Two systems are particularly important in computing because they work with powers of two, namely the "binary" and "hexadecimal" (16) systems.

Dec	Bin	Hex	Dec	Bin	Hex	Dec	Bin	Hex	Dec	Bin	Hex
0	0000	0	4	0100	4	8	1000	8	12	1100	C
1	0001	1	5	0101	5	9	1001	9	13	1101	D
2	0010	2	6	0110	6	10	1010	A	14	1110	E
3	0011	3	7	0111	7	11	1011	B	15	1111	F

From this it can be seen that each number represented by a sum of units, tens and hundreds in decimal has a similar binary pattern of units, twos, fours, eights, etc. and a hexadecimal coding of units, sixteens, and "two hundred and fifty-sixes". Conversion between the systems is easy, requiring only simple addition and subtraction; as an example, 677=1010100101=2A5. The binary and "hex" forms, containing sums of powers of two, can be stored easily in two-state stores. The example requires a ten bit register.

The standard code for characters is called the American standard code for information interchange or ASCII and uses seven bits to give 128 character codes, with an eighth bit available as a check bit. There are 32 control codes for such things as feeding lines, tabs and ringing a bell. The remaining 96 characters contain space and delete (all 1s) and 94 printable characters, which cover the decimal digits, the alphabet both upper and lower case, punctuation marks and special symbols.

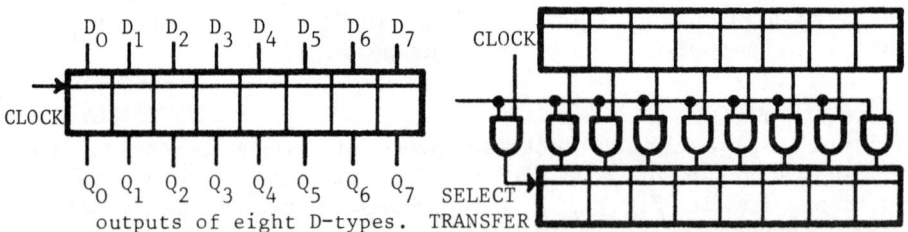

FIG. 1.10 *A REGISTER AND REGISTER TRANSFER*

Values can be set into registers just as if setting a bistable. The contents of any register, or a parallel set of inputs, can be set into another register by enabling one set of AND gates connected to its inputs and clocking the entire register. Extra logic could be added, as well as the *ENABLE* gates, between the registers, so that a function could be performed during the register transfer.

Parallel loading registers are not the only useful type. If the bits of a word are required in a serial form, for instance for transmission down telephone lines, a "shift" register is used. This is an arrangement of bistables to give bits serially on a "first in first out" (FIFO) basis or as a *QUEUE*. Fig.1.11 shows a general shift register and the "JK" bistables used have extra inputs to allow the second (slave) bistable to be set (s) or reset (r) directly. This allows the whole register to be cleared and loaded in parallel. The parallel outputs are also available and the register can be used as a serial in serial out register, a serial to parallel converter or a parallel to serial converter.

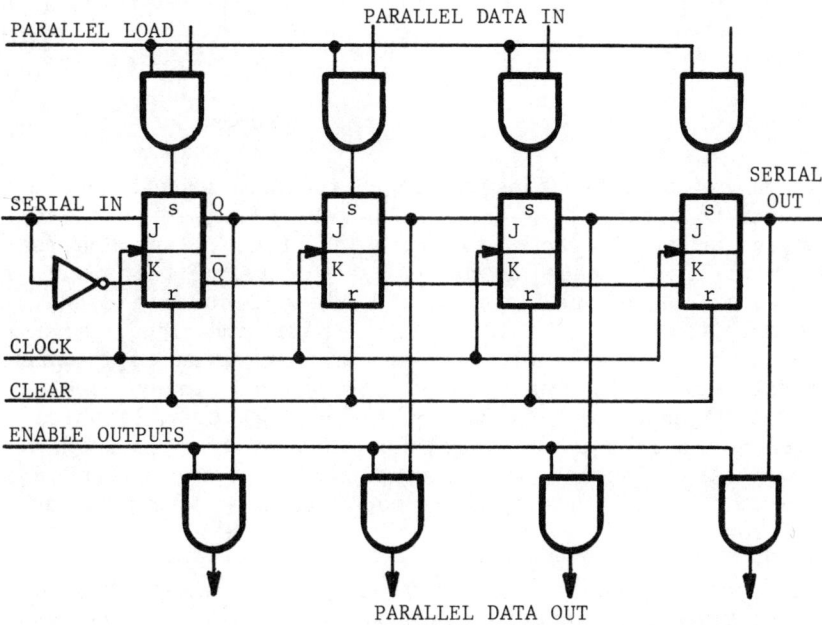

FIG. 1.11 *GENERAL SHIFT REGISTER*

A *STACK* register may be constructed from bistables which are loaded on a "last in first out" (LIFO) basis. This arrangement is usually found as a set of complete registers one word wide and many words deep. It is very useful in any application where "nesting" is needed. A word can be "pushed" onto the stack, pushing the rest of the stack down one level. Words are retrieved by "pulling" the whole stack content up one level to give a different word as the top. A useful analogy to this is a set of Russian dolls which nest one inside the other allowing only the outside one to be seen. A new doll is added by pushing it on outside the current stack of dolls, and dolls are retrieved by pulling each layer off to reveal the next. This is LIFO access.

Counters are also essential parts of computers. They are used to count occurrences of events or inputs and outputs and also produce system timing pulses when driven from a regular clock.

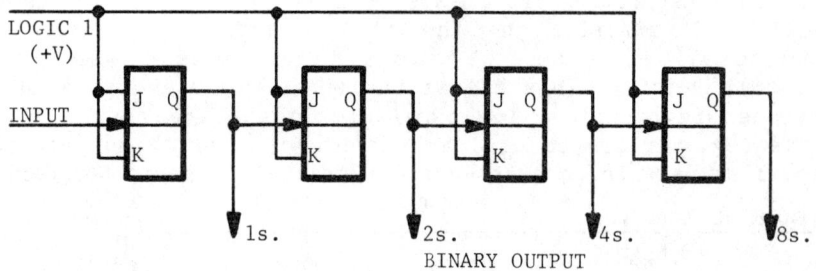

FIG. 1.12 *RIPPLE BINARY COUNTER*

A simple four-stage binary counter is shown above. This circuit can count to binary 1111 or sixteen in decimal. It contains a JK bistable for each power of two to be counted. Pulses are fed into the clock input, each complete cycle causing the first JK to "toggle" or change its output state. This produces a signal which changes at one half of the frequency of the input signal and hence counts in powers of two. The next stage which is connected similarly counts in powers of 2^2 and so on. Binary counters can be built to count to any number by adding more bistables. This counter has delays as the clock propagates or "ripples" through the bistables. Because of the rippling the outputs will not all change at the same time and the count will be wrong during these transitions.

This problem can be overcome by designing a "synchronous" counter. The clock inputs to all the bistables must be connected together so that they are all pulsed together and their outputs must change together. Fig.1.13 shows a binary counter on this principle. Each bistable has a set of conditions to allow it to toggle or not. For instance the bistable for fours is only altered when both the ones and twos bistables are set on.

BINARY OUTPUT

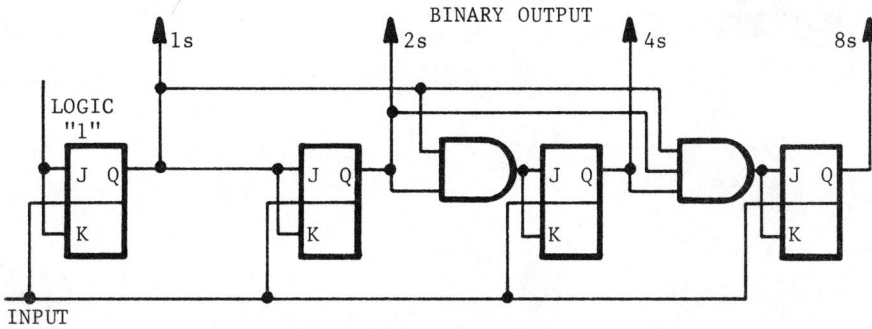

FIG. 1.13 *SYNCHRONOUS BINARY COUNTER*

In digital clocks and watches counters are used for fours, sixes and tens (60 seconds or minutes and 24 hours). A synchronous "decade" counter is shown in Fig.1.14 to illustrate the simplicity of producing a counter for any radix. This counter uses binary coded decimal (BCD) coding to count from 0000 through 0111, 1000 to 1001 (9) before resetting itself to 0000 and counting again.

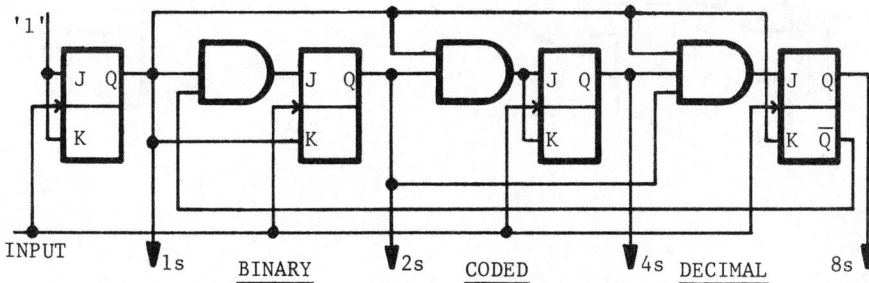

FIG. 1.14 *SYNCHRONOUS DECADE COUNTER*

2 Arithmetic Circuits

2.1 EXCLUSIVE OR AND HALF ADDITION

The basic arithmetic circuit is the exclusive OR which provides a "1" output if the two inputs are different. This is the output that is required if one adds two binary bits. The Boolean expression for the exclusive OR is thus: $T=\{A \wedge B^{\neg}\} \vee \{A^{\neg} \wedge B\}$ or $T=A \oplus B$. To complete the picture for adding two bits, we will need to generate a carry if the inputs are both "1", that is if $C=A \wedge B$. The combination of these two parts is called a half adder. The half adder will add single bits, but it is not sufficient to add complete binary numbers as it takes no account of a carry into the stage from a previous stage.

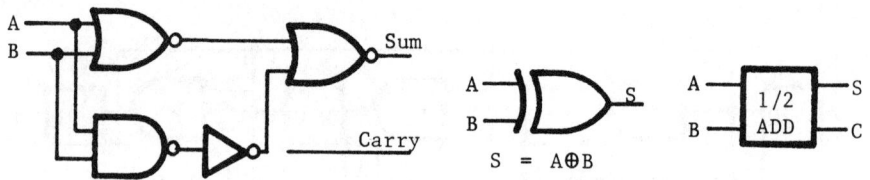

$$S = A \oplus B$$

FIG. 2.1 *EXCLUSIVE OR AND HALF ADDER*

A full adder circuit is required. It has three inputs, the two bits to be added and a carry in from the previous stage. It produces a sum and a carry out to the next stage. Its Boolean equations after minimisation are:

$$S=A \wedge B \wedge C \vee A^{\neg} \wedge B^{\neg} \wedge C \vee A^{\neg} \wedge B \wedge C^{\neg} \vee A \wedge B^{\neg} \wedge C^{\neg} \quad \text{and} \quad C=A \wedge B \vee B \wedge C \vee C \wedge A$$

for sum and carry. This could be implemented using 9 gates and 3 inverters, giving the form with minimum delay.

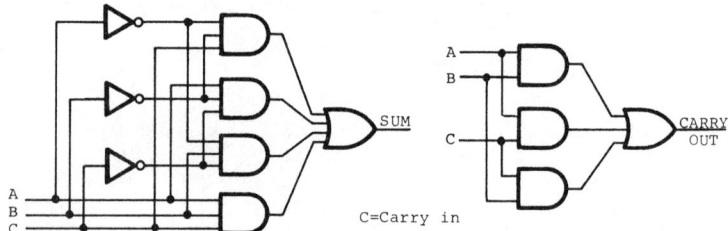

C=Carry in

FIG. 2.2 *FULL ADDER CIRCUIT*

Any combinational function can be implemented in this way, giving a maximum delay of three gates. It can be implemented using fewer components if a greater delay is accepted. Using this method the circuit is made of half adders. Let $H=A{\wedge}B^{\neg}{\vee}A^{\neg}{\wedge}B$ and $K=A{\wedge}B$. Then it can be seen that the sum and carry outputs of a full adder are $SUM=C{\wedge}H^{\neg}{\vee}C^{\neg}{\wedge}H$ and $CARRY=K{\vee}C{\wedge}H$, which gives an implementation of two half adders and one OR gate. This will be cheaper but slower and would not be satisfactory in fast machines. The addition of two complete binary numbers is performed using the basic full adder, either in parallel or serially.

2.2   SERIAL ADDITION

A full "n" bit serial adder uses one full adder circuit, shown implemented using the half adder approach in Fig.2.3. Two bits, from shift registers, and the previous carry are presented to it at each clock time. The full adder circuit produces a sum bit and a carry, which is held, to replace the previous carry once the sum bit has been stored. The serial adder has the advantage of very low cost, but the disadvantage of slow speed, as the total add time is approximately the product of the delay through the adder and carry store, times the number of bits in the word.

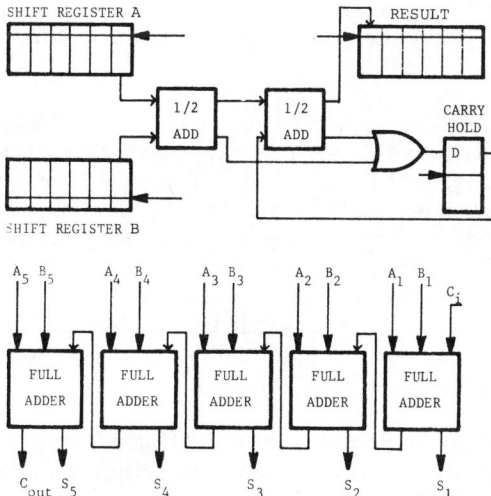

FIG. 2.3 *SERIAL AND PARALLEL ADDITION*

2.3   PARALLEL ADDITION

By using "n" full adder circuits for an "n" bit word, a full parallel adder can be devised. The carry is now connected straight to the next stage and the minimum delay is one adder stage. However, many carries may be generated and they will have to *RIPPLE* through some stages. This would slow the adder, to give a total add time of the delay through the full adder multiplied by the number of adjacent stages producing carries. A method of reducing even this delay is described further on.

2.4   SUBTRACTION

It is possible to design a "subtractor" in a similar way to an adder, from the truth table for subtraction, having "borrows" instead of carries. If a representation of the numbers used one bit for the sign, leaving the rest for the magnitude, then an exclusive OR of the sign bits of the two numbers would switch in either the adder or the subtractor. This system has a disadvantage, namely that both -0 and +0 exist as different bit patterns. A review of number representation will help to solve the dilemma.

2.5   NUMBER REPRESENTATION

There are many ways of representing numbers in the store and registers inside a computer. Some of these have significant advantages. Samples of the important representations (using five bits) are shown in Fig.2.4.

MAGNITUDE ONLY: If integers with positive values only are required, then a straightforward translation of the decimal number into binary may be used, giving a range of 0 to 2^n-1 for n bits.

SIGN AND MAGNITUDE: It would be useful to have numbers which could be negative as well as positive and the sign and magnitude representation suggested above is the obvious way to achieve this. A bit, say the most significant, is used to signify the sign (+ or -) and the rest signify the magnitude. The range is then $\pm 2^{n-1}-1$. The immediate disadvantages are that +0 and -0 exist as separate numbers, which will be very confusing for the user, and that special logic will be needed to handle the signs and to decide whether to use an adder or subtractor, even though "add" or "subtract" was specified (A--B=A+B).

COMPLEMENT FORMS: For any number "c", if two numbers "p" and "q" are such that c=p+q, then p and q are said to be complementary with respect to c. For a computer with "n" bit words, "x" and 2^n-x are complementary with respect to 2^n. This is the two's complement. In this form, if "x" is a number, then -x is represented by 2^n-x. If the straight complement (change all 1's for 0's and vice versa) is formed then this is the one's complement and it can be seen that the representation of numbers in this form is 1 less than the 2's complement form. Hence a 2's complement can be formed by inverting a number and adding one in the least significant position. The 1's complement form has the disadvantage that both +0 and -0 exist. Also it does not represent a true negative, as x+-x≠0, but equals -0. Addition requires an end around carry to cope with this.

5 BITS	INTEGER				FLOATING POINT		
Binary	Magnit only	Sign & magnit	One's comp	Two's comp	Biased expt	2sComp mant	Range
01111	15	+15	+15	+15	- 1	+15/16	P
01110	14	+14	+14	+14	- 2	+ 7/8	O N
01101	13	+13	+13	+13	- 3	+13/16	S O
01100	12	+12	+12	+12	- 4	+ 3/4	I R
01011	11	+11	+11	+11	- 5	+11/16	T M
01010	10	+10	+10	+10	- 6	+ 5/8	I A
01001	9	+ 9	+ 9	+ 9	- 7	+ 9/16	V L
01000	8	+ 8	+ 8	+ 8	- 8	+ 1/2	E
00111	7	+ 7	+ 7	+ 7	- 9	+ 7/16	P
00110	6	+ 6	+ 6	+ 6	-10	+ 3/8	O U
00101	5	+ 5	+ 5	+ 5	-11	+ 5/16	S N
00100	4	+ 4	+ 4	+ 4	-12	+ 1/4	T D
00011	3	+ 3	+ 3	+ 3	-13	+ 3/16	I E
00010	2	+ 2	+ 2	+ 2	-14	+ 1/8	V R
00001	1	+ 1	+ 1	+ 1	-15	+ 1/16	E
00000	0	+ 0	+ 0	0	-16	0	zero
11111	31	-15	- 0	- 1	+15	- 1/16	N
11110	30	-14	- 1	- 2	+14	- 1/8	E U
11101	29	-13	- 2	- 3	+13	- 3/16	G N
11100	28	-12	- 3	- 4	+12	- 1/4	A D
11011	27	-11	- 4	- 5	+11	- 5/16	T E
11010	26	-10	- 5	- 6	+10	- 3/8	I R
11001	25	- 9	- 6	- 7	+ 9	- 7/16	V
11000	24	- 8	- 7	- 8	+ 8	- 1/2	E
10111	23	- 7	- 8	- 9	+ 7	- 9/16	N
10110	22	- 6	- 9	-10	+ 6	- 5/8	E N
10101	21	- 5	-10	-11	+ 5	-11/16	G O
10100	20	- 4	-11	-12	+ 4	- 3/4	A R
10011	19	- 3	-12	-13	+ 3	-13/16	T M
10010	18	- 2	-13	-14	+ 2	- 7/8	I A
10001	17	- 1	-14	-15	+ 1	-15/16	V L
10000	16	- 0	-15	-16	0	- 1	E

FIG. 2.4 NUMBER REPRESENTATION

TWO'S COMPLEMENT: This is a true negative as x+-x=0, so an adder will subtract if presented with a pair of numbers of different sign, without any alteration to its logic. This representation has a unique zero and the negative of a number is very easily created. The two's complement is almost universally used, to represent signed integers, in computers. The range of

1's complement is the same as for sign and magnitude, but for 2's complement, as there is only one zero, the range is assymetric, and from -2^{n-1} to $+2^{n-1}-1$.

FLOATING POINT: Real numbers require both a magnitude, and an exponent, i.e. 2.479×10^{27} has a magnitude of 2.479 and an exponent of 27. Both the mantissa and exponent could be negative or positive, so two registers using two's complement forms could be used. In normal practice, however, it is found that the algorithms for floating point operations are easier if there is a continuous representation for the exponent. Note that, at zero, there is a discontinuity in the 2's complement form.

BIASED EXPONENT: The method adopted for coping with this is to take the range of numbers, say -2^{n-1} to $+2^{n-1}-1$, and map this to the run of binary numbers (00000 to 11111 in the five bit examples), giving a form where zero appears as the mid point of the range of binary numbers. This is the same as taking all numbers and adding one half of the total range to them, such that -2^{n-1} is represented by what would have been zero, zero is represented by half the range (2^{n-1}) and the maximum possible positive number is represented by the maximum magnitude only form. This means that we can shift numbers up and down bit by bit without worrying about passing through zero. It is normal practice to use a biased exponent form and a 2's complement mantissa form for representing floating point numbers. The mantissa is used to represent a fraction (in binary) which is multiplied by the power of two given in the exponent to get the actual number. The range of the mantissa is thus from -1.0 to $+(2^{n-1}-1)/(2^{n-1})$, i.e. -1 to $+0.9375$ in five bits.

The range of the exponent is $2^{-2^{n-1}}$ to $2^{(2^{n-1}-1)}$, i.e. between 0.00001526 times and 32768 times the mantissa. It is usual to hold floating point mantissae in a *NORMALISED* form so that the greatest number of significant bits can be retained; the range of these is shown in the example. See Chapter three for more details of floating point operations and normalisation. The fractional form of the mantissa is:

$$a.2^{-1}+b.2^{-2}+c.2^{-3}+d.2^{-4}+\ldots\ldots\ldots x.2^{-n}$$

Note that in two's complement form the sign of a number is indicated by the most significant bit, but that this is not a "sign bit". The same occurs for the biased form, but the bit is the inverse indication (1 for + and 0 for -).

2.6   CARRY PREDICTION FOR AN ADDER

In a machine with a large word, permitting carries to ripple through could be fairly slow. To avoid this, it is usual to use carry prediction, to predict the "carry in" to a given stage instead of computing the carry out from a stage and using this as the carry into the next stage. We define a carry generate and a carry propagate for each stage of the adder:

A stage GENERATES a carry when $G_i = A_i \wedge B_i$ for stage i

A stage PROPAGATES a carry when $P_i = A_i \oplus B_i$ for stage i

hence the "1" carry for the Kth stage is:

$$C_k = G_k \vee P_k \wedge C_{k-1} = G_k \vee (P_k \wedge (G_{k-1} \vee P_{k-1} \wedge C_{k-2}))$$

Thus if one defines $G_0 = C_0$, then the expression for the carry from the Kth stage (into the $K+1^{th}$) becomes:

$$C_k = G_k \vee (\prod_{i=k}^{k} P_i) \wedge G_{k-1} \vee (\prod_{i=k-1}^{k} P_i) \wedge G_{k-2} \cdots \cdots \vee (\prod_{i=1}^{k} P_i) \wedge G_0$$

$$\text{where} \quad (\prod_{i=k-n}^{k} P_i) = P_k \wedge P_{k-1} \wedge P_{k-2} \cdots \wedge P_{k-n}$$

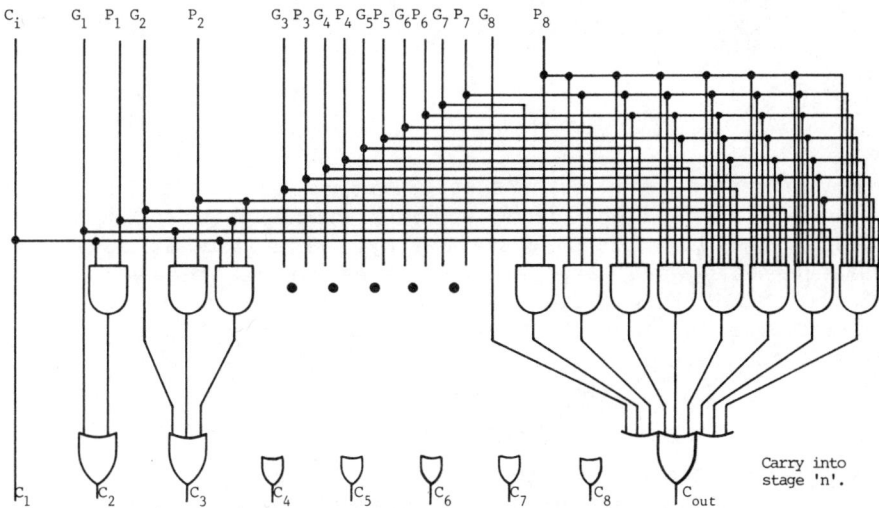

FIG. 2.5 *EIGHT BIT CARRY PREDICTION LOGIC*

This could be implemented directly in three levels of logic, so the total delay of the adder would be 6 gates. This is not normally practicable due to the large cost: consider the last term for a 60 bit word. It can be shown that the probability of a ripple occurring over 8 or more bits is very low, thus most designs tend to use carry prediction over blocks of 8 bits, as shown in Fig.2.5, and permit rippling between blocks, or use two (or more) levels of prediction. In the latter case prediction would be done over say 8 bits and then the remaining carries between blocks have the same treatment to predict if a carry would ripple through the whole block.

The full carry predicting adder produces the generate and propagate terms using half adder circuits, working in parallel. The predicted carry and the two bit sum from the half adder are combined using an exclusive OR for each stage. An eight bit implementation is shown in Fig.2.6 and the carry predict logic has to be included as shown.

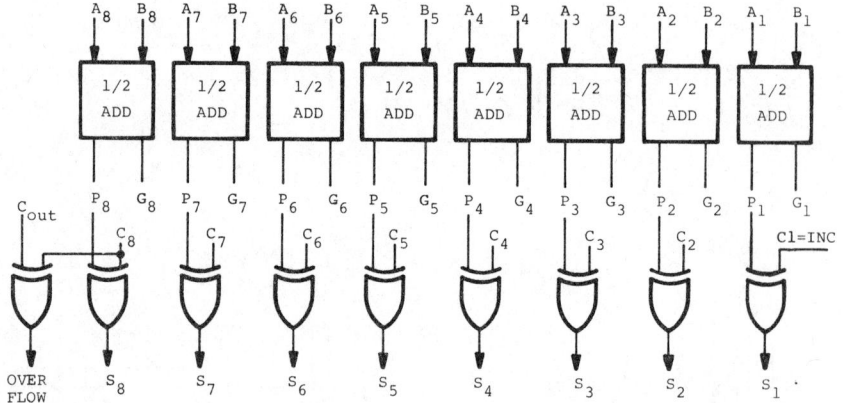

FIG. 2.6 FULL CARRY PREDICT ADDER

The largest integer numbers which may be held in a 16 bit word are +32767 and -32768, using a two's complement representation. If, as the result of an operation by the arithmetic logic, for instance adding two large numbers, a result is produced which is outside these limits, then an OVERFLOW has occurred. This gives an erroneous result and its occurrence is detected by a little extra logic, also shown in Fig.2.6. The condition for overflow is:

$$C_{out} \wedge \overline{C_n} \vee \overline{C_{out}} \wedge C_n = 1$$

where "C_n" is the carry into the last bit and "C_{out}" is the carry produced from the last bit (quasi-sign bit). It is not possible to produce an overflow if the signs of the two input numbers are the same for subtraction, or different for addition.

3 Arithmetic and Logic Unit

3.1 SIMPLE LOGICAL FUNCTIONS

The ALU will contain simple logical functions, such as AND, OR,
exclusive OR, and also other functions for shifting or rotating a
word held in a register. Test facilities for comparison with
constants such as 0, -, +, etc. the results being flags set true
or false for checking by the control unit, will be of great use
and are shown in Fig.3.1.

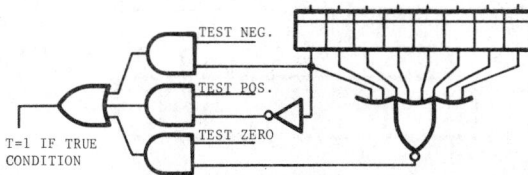

FIG. 3.1 *TESTING FOR ZERO, PLUS OR MINUS*

3.2 ROTATING AND SHIFTING

It is useful to be able to shift words right or left by one or
more bits, either to locate certain bits or groups of bits in a
given place, say the least significant end of the word, or to
effectively divide or multiply the number by 2 for each one bit
shift. If bits are to be moved up or down in a word and no loss
of bits may be tolerated, for instance if the bits represent
logical values, flags, or characters, then a *ROTATE* is used. This
"wraps around" the least significant and most significant ends of
a register such that if a bit is shifted out of one end, it
shifts back into the other. Rotating may go in either direction.
Sometimes an extra bistable, called a *LINK*, is added. This is
connected in the path between the ends of the register so that a
bit rotated off one end goes into the link and the link content
goes into the other end of the register, as in Fig.3.2. Rotates
may then be specified as left/right and with/without link.
Rotating does not preserve numeric forms, only logical and
character representations. As with decimal numbers, where moving
the decimal point divides or multiplies by 10, it would be
expected that shifting a binary number would divide or multiply
by 2. Rotation obviously does not perform this, but an arithmetic
shift does. In an arithmetic shift, a shift to the left will

multiply by 2 if zeros are fed into the least significant end. For example, 00110 is six 01100 is twelve, and with five bits and two's complement representation, 11010 is minus six and 10100 is minus twelve. A shift to the right implies division by 2 and, as can easily be seen, shifting in zeros to the most significant end maintains the correct answer for positive numbers. The example above for negative numbers, however, shows that ones will have to be fed in to replace bits shifted down to the right to retain the correct negative representation. In practice, the most significant bit is duplicated in the bit it is shifted to, and in itself as the sign bit, for an arithmetic shift.

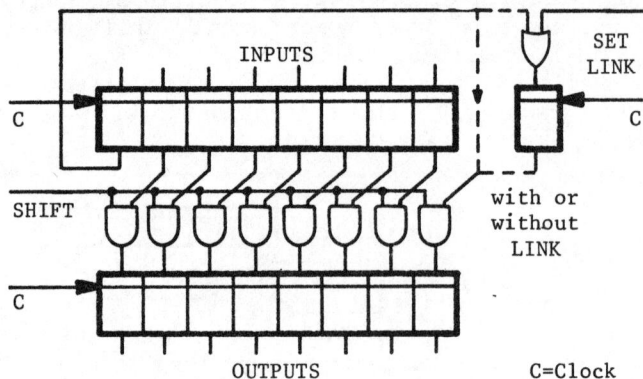

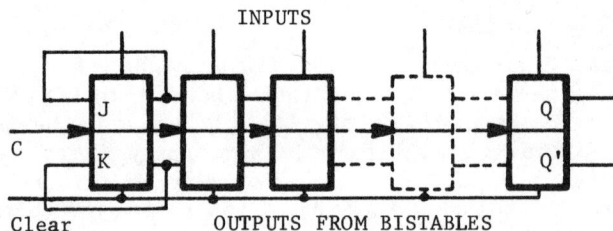

FIG. 3.2 PARALLEL ROTATE AND SERIAL SHIFT

The logical shift, in which zeros are fed in at either end, is little used, since the same result is achieved in three cases by the arithmetic shift and the same result can be achieved in all four cases using a rotate with link, clearing the link between each bit shift.

Shift registers could be used for all these methods, instead of register transfers, see Fig.3.2, but the structure of the rest of the arithmetic and logic unit and of the control unit normally uses register transfers, so they are more normal for shifting. Also, if instructions are available for multiple shifts, they may be done in parallel by having other sets of AND gates going from each bit of the input register to the relevant bit of the output register.

3.3 COMPARING AND MASKING

It is necessary in many computations to know whether a number is positive, negative or zero, to decrement a count of cycles through a sequence of instructions until zero is reached, or to compare two numbers, characters, etc. to see if they are the same. The latter could be accomplished by subtracting one from the other and testing to see if the result was zero, or positive for greater than, or negative for less than. A simpler method for testing two registers for the same content is described further on. Fig.3.1 shows the arrangement for testing a word for zero (all zero bits) and for testing the sign, positive or negative. If a two's complement representation is used for integers and mantissae of real numbers, then a positive number has a zero sign bit and a negative number a 1 sign bit. For a biased exponent form, the sign bit is reversed so that a positive exponent has a "1" sign bit and a negative exponent a "0" sign bit.

The comparison of two registers involves an exclusive OR between each bit of one register and the corresponding bit of the other register, and then an OR of the outputs of all these. A zero output implies the words are the same, whether they represent numbers, characters or logical flags. As a carry predict adder "propogate" function is an exclusive OR between the required bits of the input words, the only addition is the multi-input OR gate.

A part of a word may be required on its own, with the rest of the word zero, so that it may be compared or used in isolation. This is accomplished by masking one register by another. A pattern of bits, with ones set where the content is required and zero for the parts to be masked over, is held. The AND function is performed between corresponding bits of this *MASK* and the word to be masked. If, for instance, two characters are held in a word, they can be placed in turn in the least significant end of a register by a mask and a rotation.

3.4 ACCUMULATION AND GENERAL REGISTERS

As has been seen, registers are made from a number of bistables and are arranged so as to hold the value of a machine word. The registers have suitable input and output gating to load new contents, or to use the current contents as input to some other logic. A particular case of a register is an *ACCUMULATOR*. The results produced from arithmetic and logical functions reside in an accumulator. The accumulator can be considered as the resting place of the currently accumulated result. In small machines functions are performed between a location in store and an accumulator, with the result overwriting an accumulator. Machines can have many accumulators, in which case they require a mechanism to decide which is used for a given instruction.

3.5   MULTIPLICATION AND DIVISION

The simplest method of multiplication for a computer would be to load the multiplicand into two registers and add them together for the number of times given by the multiplier, however this is obviously very slow for large multipliers. As an alternative, elements which have a logarithmic transfer function due to their physical nature can be constructed. Two values could be passed through logarithmic elements and then added, with the result being passed through an inverse logarithmic unit to give the answer. This method has the disadvantage of requiring the logarithmic elements to be very stable as they are analog components. Yet another technique could be to use elements with a square law response, due to their physical properties, and the "quarter square technique" which relies on the relationship $XY = 1/4((X+Y)^2 - (X-Y)^2)$ using addition and subtraction only. This has the same drawback; square law devices are essentially analog in operation and thus need to be stable over long periods of time to be satisfactory for a digital computer. These techniques are not often used.

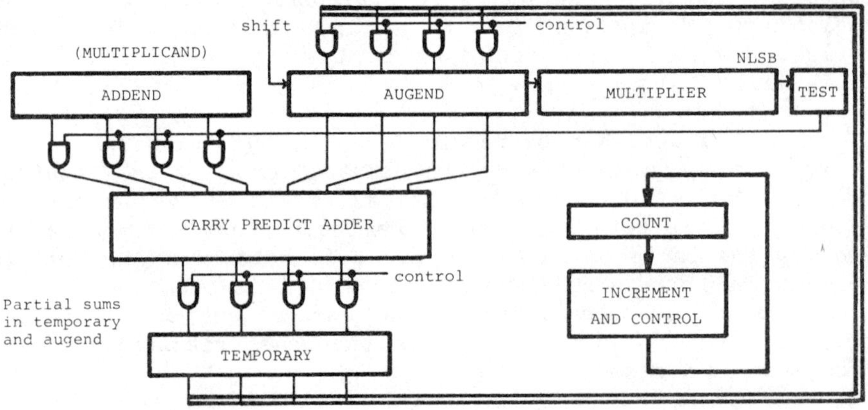

FIG. 3.3 *MULTIPLICATION WITHOUT SIGN*

The normal method is derived from a techique similar to that used for long multiplication in schools, namely to take one digit of the multiplier at a time, multiply the multiplicand by it and add this number to the accumulated partial result, then shifting to the next digit and also shifting the partial result (by writing an extra zero). In binary multiplication each digit can only be a "0" or a "1", so multiplying the multiplicand by the digit can only give an answer zero if the digit is "0" or the multiplicand if the digit is "1". Assuming an equal length multiplier and multiplicand, which is likely to be the word length of the machine, a simplified form of the algorithm using the logic shown in Fig.3.3 follows.

0. Set a COUNT to the number of digits in the multiplier.
1. Clear the AUGEND and the TEMPORARY registers.
2. Set the multiplier in the MULTIPLIER register.
3. Set the multiplicand in the ADDEND register.
4. If *TEST* is one add ADDEND to AUGEND;
   if *TEST* is zero add nothing to AUGEND;
   place the result in TEMPORARY.
5. Transfer TEMPORARY to AUGEND.
6. Shift (arithmetic) AUGEND:MULTIPLIER:TEST 1 bit right.
7. Decrement COUNT, if positive repeat from 4;
   if zero stop with result in AUGEND:MULTIPLIER.

This method is very satisfactory, particularly if a carry predict adder is used. However it only multiplies positive numbers and as numbers may be negative, a small modification to the algorithm is required. Assuming that negative numbers are held in a two's complement form, a more complex test is substituted at stage "4". The test bit and the next least significant bit (*NLSB*) of the multiplier are compared, to determine the action.

4. If *TEST* is zero and *NLSB* is one add ADDEND to AUGEND; if *TEST* is one and *NLSB* is zero subtract ADDEND from AUGEND; if *TEST* and *NLSB* are the same add AUGEND to zero; place the result in TEMPORARY.

The logic of Fig.3.3 has to be changed to allow selection of addition or subtraction and it is important to note that the shifts are arithmetic, to preserve the sign of the partial result at any stage. Additional action is required at the end to clear the sign bit of the multiplier and leave the double length result. This method, known as Booth's algorithm, is the one normally used in small computers, though it does fail if the multiplier is minus one (i.e. 111...111). This is tested for seperately and the correct answer substituted.

Higher speed techniques for larger machines work by carrying out all the tests and additions or subtractions (required for each multiplier bit) in parallel, instead of serially. A test mechanism, shifter and full adder are required for each bit of the multiplier word, with an obvious increase in cost.

Division is performed by analogous methods, but in place of shifting right and adding, one shifts left and subtracts, performing the tests at the most significant end of the divisor. There is an additional problem with integer division, namely division by, or into, zero, which should give defined results of infinity or zero. These results are not yielded by the algorithms used, so separate tests are made, with exceptions being signalled.

3.6   FLOATING POINT ADDITION

This can be performed by an algorithm, implemented by hardware in large machines, or software, or in "firmware" on smaller micro-controlled machines, a technique which is discussed in Chapter five. With two numbers (a,A) and (b,B) where a,b are the exponents, A,B the mantissae, the first operation is to pre-scale. This forces the numbers to the same exponent by altering the mantissa. They can then be added, with some checks being performed to ensure the result is meaningful.

PRE-SCALING If a>b shift B right k places and increment b,k times where k=a-b. If a<b shift A right k places and increment a,k times where k=b-a. If a=b no action.

ADDITION OR SUBTRACTION A:=A+B (or A-B as a two's complement form is used).

POST-NORMALISATION If A above range shift A 1 place right, a:=a+1 If A below range shift A 1 place left, a:=a-1 and repeat test. If A in range no action. The *RANGE* conditions are:

$A_n \wedge \overline{A_{n-1}} \vee \overline{A_n} \wedge A_{n-1}$ =1 if in range =0 if below range

$C_{out} \wedge \overline{C_n} \vee \overline{C_{out}} \wedge C_n$ =1 if above range

A_n and A_{n-1} are the two most significant bits of the result, and C_n and C_{out} are the carries into and out of the most significant bit of the addition. The above range condition is the same as the overflow condition for integers.

EXCEPTION CHECKS Examine "a" for *UNDERFLOW*, i.e. below possible values. Set (a,A) to zero, though it can be advantageous to signal an exception and give the programmer the significant parts of the result at this point, rather than setting (a,A)=0. Examine "a" for *OVERFLOW*, i.e. number too large to hold. Set the overflow exception indicator.

FIG. 3.4 *FLOATING POINT ADDITION*

3.7   OTHER FLOATING POINT OPERATIONS

The algorithm for floating point multiplication is simpler as it is only necessary to add the two exponents (a+b) and multiply the two mantissae (AxB), then to post normalise to adjust the *RANGE* and check the *FLOW* as for addition. Division of floating point numbers is the same except that the exponents are subtracted and the mantissae divided. The advantage of two´s complement form for the mantissae has already been shown and it is clear that a representation which has its discontinuity at its extremities, rather than at zero, will be preferable for the exponent. Incrementing and decrementing the exponent will be no problem and the discontinuity will detect only exception conditions. The biased exponent form is preferred in most small machines.

Though binary arithmetic has been discussed, there are other possible bases to use. Decimal arithmetic, though convenient for humans, is most unsuitable for machines, but hexadecimal, or base 16, arithmetic fits neatly into powers of two and hence onto two state (bistable) logic. The advantage of using a larger base is that, though the algorithms are more complex, less normalisation is required, as the normalised range of numbers is greater. For example, using positive unsigned fractions, the binary normalised range is from 1/2 to almost 1, whereas the decimal normalised range is from 1/10 to almost 1 and the hexadecimal from 1/16 to almost 1. Large machines would also include functions such as sine and cosine and some of the hyperbolic functions, though they would always be performed by software on minicomputers.

Conversion between fixed and floating point representations is also required. Obviously this is only possible from "float" to "fix" when the integer value produced fits in the computer word.

4 Control Circuits

4.1   DECODING AND TIMING CIRCUITS

The arithmetic and logic unit will have a number of different
functions, which it can perform on its inputs, any result being
placed in an accumulator. It will be necessary to have a number
of lines to select which function is active or enabled. It is
usual to encode these lines to minimise the number of bits to be
stored. This code is known as the function code or *OPERATION
CODE*. The length of this OP code will vary from 3 bits in the
simplest machines to 12 or more bits in large machines with very
many functions. The operation code is decoded when required, to
enable the correct function (add, multiply, shift, etc.) and the
correct parts of the arithmetic and logic unit.

   The machine described below has a 16 bit word, with three bits
reserved for the OP code. A decoder like that shown in Fig.4.1
would take the OP code and produce individual control signals for
each instruction. Such a decoder used to be constructed from a
matrix of diodes and is often referred to as a decoding matrix.

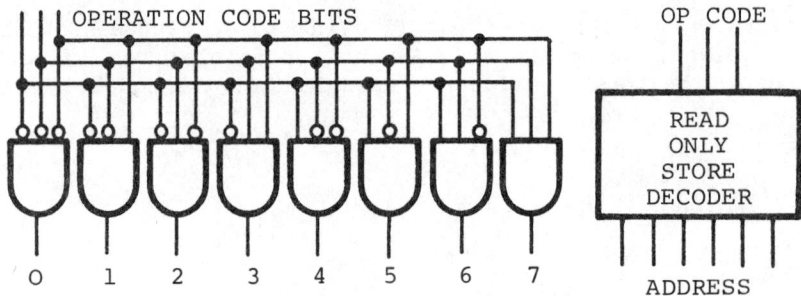

FIG. 4.1 *DECODING CIRCUITS*

   In more complex control units it will be necessary to have a
number, or address rather than a single control line, as the
output of the decoder. This is achieved by using a read only
store to hold the numbers, with the one required being chosen by
the individual control line. Having determined the function,
timing control will be required to ensure that the various
individual steps which make up the instruction are performed at
the correct time. A single pulse of width "t" nanoseconds is

easily generated using the circuit of Fig.4.2a.

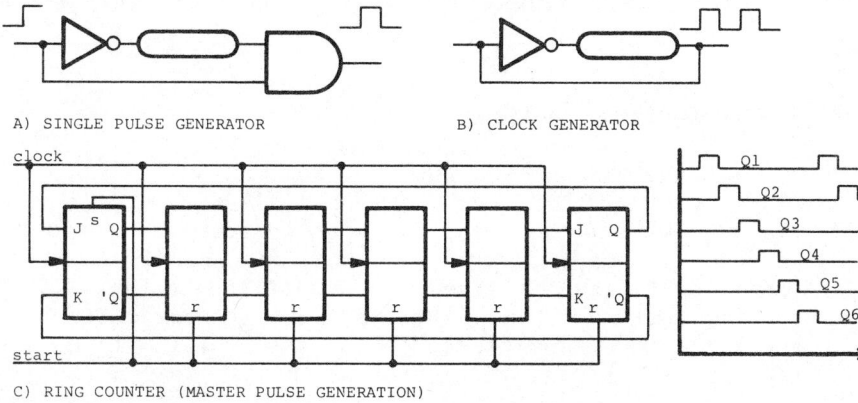

A) SINGLE PULSE GENERATOR

B) CLOCK GENERATOR

C) RING COUNTER (MASTER PULSE GENERATION)

FIG. 4.2 TIMING AND PULSE GENERATION

A delay element of time "t" is required, and this could be formed simply from a piece of wire, as electrons travel at a speed close to that of light. A nanosecond, 10^{-9} seconds, is the delay of nine inches of ordinary wire! A continuous stream of pulses (a "clock") is also easily produced, as shown, if a delay element of the right amount is available. To give the separate lines with pulses at defined, different times, the "clock" pulse stream is fed into a "ring counter". This is a shift register connected so that it wraps around its outputs into its inputs. It is started with a single bit in stage one and this bit is shifted down the register one place at each clock pulse. The timing diagram shown in Fig.4.2 gives the output from each stage and, as can be seen, the control can cycle continuously, performing operations at the specified times.

4.2   FIXED WIRE CONTROL CIRCUITS

The basic cycle of a stored program machine is *FETCH*, then *EXECUTE*, and the control unit will have to follow this cycle. With an arithmetic and logic unit described previously and its accumulators, a store with a simple access mechanism, an instruction register and program counter, we can produce a "hardwired" control unit as in Fig.4.3. All the paths along which instructions and data move are shown and control is effected by parallel sets of gates, to enable chosen paths at a given time. This is described in Section 4.4.

This control system has the registers and "black boxes" of logic circuitry listed below. The mnemonic names of registers are those on Fig.4.3.

"A" the accumulator register.

"B" the storage buffer register.

"S" the storage address register. When an address is put in the storage address register and the command "read" or "write" is given, a copy of the content of the location specified is put into the storage buffer register (read), or the content of the storage buffer register is put into the location (write).

"I" the instruction register which holds the current instruction being executed.

"C" the program counter, which holds the address of the next instruction to be fetched.

"R" the temporary result register.

STORE, a storage unit accessed as described above via the storage address and buffer registers.

ALU, arithmetic and logic unit, performs the function, decoded from the OP-code in the instruction, on the "A" and "B" registers, and puts the result in the "R" register.

DECODE, the Instruction OP-code decoder, determines which operation or sequence of operations is required.

CLOCK, a master timing device to control the timing of the machine and its operations.

INC, a unit to increment the program counter. This could be done using the arithmetic and logic unit, but it is shown separately for clarity.

CONSOLE KEYS

PROGRAM
COUNT

COUNT
INCREMENT

This symbol is used
to represent sets of
16 enable gates. All
lines are 16 bits
except where shown.

STORE
ADDRESS

TP

CLOCK ── TP

STORE

READ

WRITE

TIMING
SIGNALS

ACCUMULATOR

STORE
BUFFER

INSTRUCTION

op	I	address
3	1	12

ARITHMETIC
AND
LOGIC
UNIT

FUNCTION
SELECT
ADD, SHR
etcetera

DECODE

CONTROL SIGNALS
(see Fig.4.6)

TEMP **R**ESULT

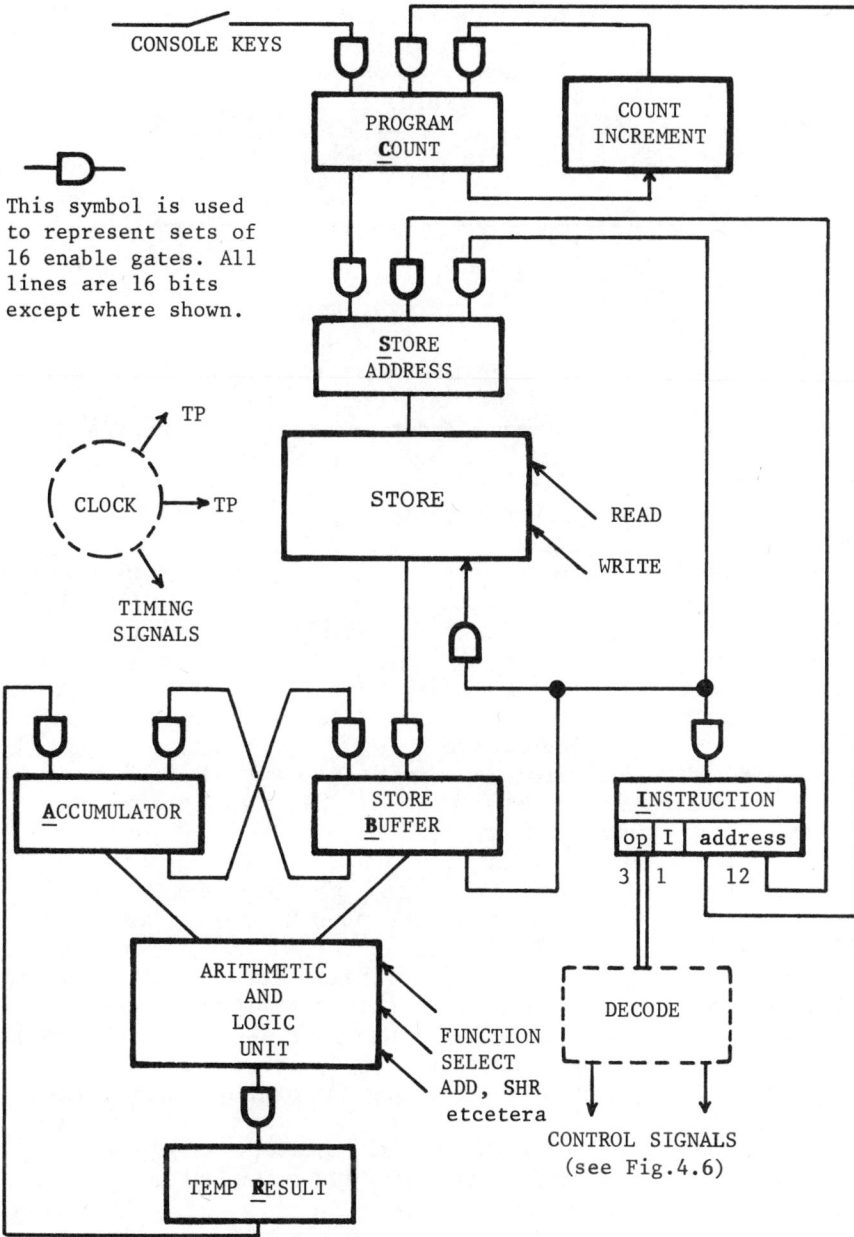

FIG. 4.3 *FIXED WIRE CONTROL UNIT*

4.3   INSTRUCTION FORMAT AND INSTRUCTION SET

The format of instructions varies and each range of machines has
its own instruction formats and its own set of instructions. As a
very simple example, consider a machine with a 16 bit word and a
64K word store. Thus all 16 bits will be needed to give access to
the whole of the store. However, an OP code is needed and only 12
bits are used for the *ADDRESS* field, after using 1 bit to give us
an escape to get at more than the 4096 words that 12 bits will
address. This will be described later. Three bits are left for
the OP code.

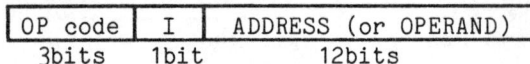

OP code	I	ADDRESS (or OPERAND)
3bits	1bit	12bits

FIG. 4.4 INSTRUCTION FORMAT

The instruction set for the simple machine described is
necessarily limited to 8 basic instructions, but this can be
expanded by having an OP code function where the address bits do
not represent an address, but some other *OPERAND*. This operand
will provide extensions and alterations to the original
instruction. One example of this type of "immediate" instruction
is the execute input output (XIO), where a storage address is not
needed and so the operand can contain the device number and the
function or status information. Another example is the operate
(OPR) group of instructions, in which the operation to be
performed does not require a storage address and the operand
field indicates which of the group is to be performed.
Instructions which have implicit addresses, such as complement
accumulator, shift accumulator left or right, skip next
instruction if accumulator is zero (or + or -) fall into this
group. This limited instruction set has sufficient codes to
perform all the operations required.

The bit number shown for each of the operate group of
instructions is the position in the operand field which must be
set. All zero in the operand field is a NOP or no operation
instruction, which does nothing and takes an instruction time to
do it. In practice this is useful, though at first sight it seems
unnecessary. Two operations may happen at one time if they are
not conflicting. For instance, to "two's complement" the
accumulator, CMA and INC are selected together. This implies an
order of precedence in which the bits are checked and the
operations performed. Skip on accumulator negative can be
achieved by SKP and SPA, and skip if accumulator non-zero is
arranged similarly.

OP code	Number	Description
BRA n	000	Branch to the location specified by the address field.
BRS n	001	Branch to the subroutine starting at the address specified.
ADD n	010	Add the contents of location "n" to the accumulator, leaving the result in the accumulator.
XOR n	011	Exclusively OR the contents of location "n" with the accumulator, leaving the result in the accumulator.
AND n	100	And the contents of location "n" with the accumulator, leaving the result in the accumulator.
STO n	101	Store the accumulator contents in "n", leaving the accumulator as it was.
XIO d,f	110	Execute the input output function "f" on device "d" (write register to printer).
OPR x	111	Operate the immediate instruction from the list below, specified by "x".

OPR code	Bit	Description
CLA	4	Clear the accumulator.
CMA	5	Complement (invert) the accumulator.
INC	6	Increment the accumulator.
SHR	7	Shift the accumulator 1 bit to the right arithmetically.
SHL	8	Shift the accumulator 1 bit to the left arithmetically.
RWR	9	Rotate the accumulator 1 bit to the right with the link.
RWL	10	Rotate the accumulator 1 bit to the left with the link.
SKP	11	Skip the next instruction.
SZA	12	Skip the next instruction if the content of the accumulator is zero.
SPA	13	Skip the next instruction if the accumulator is positive (sign bit=0).
SZL	14	Skip the next instruction if the link is zero.
CLL	15	Clear the link.

FIG. 4.5 *SIMPLE INSTRUCTION SET*

4.4   COMMAND GENERATION

To commence operation, the start address of a program in the store is put into the program counter "C" by switches. The timing generator is started and this starts the machine cycling through its time states. The machine described has 12 bistables in its ring counter, so there are 12 time pulses per instruction. The timing described is for a fixed cycle synchronous machine (no one would ever build one!) because it is easier to visualise. All the steps happen at fixed, specified times in the cycle. Asynchronous machines perform all the same steps, in the same order, but they happen at unspecified times. The number of steps in the most complicated instruction in the example determines the number of intermediate time pulses.

The *FETCH* part of the cycle is very simple and takes the first four pulses of every main cycle. The contents of the program counter "C" are transferred to the store address register "S". The store is given the "read" pulse, it gets the required content and puts it in the store buffer "B". The program counter content is incremented to point to the next instruction and the fetch is completed by transferring the content of the store buffer (which is the instruction) to the instruction register "I". An instruction in the "I" register is decoded and so one of the control lines will be true, say the ADD line. All subsequent time pulses for this cycle are gated with the control lines in the form of a "command generator". Hence time pulse 6 AND function ADD causes a particular operation to occur, or register transfer to take place.

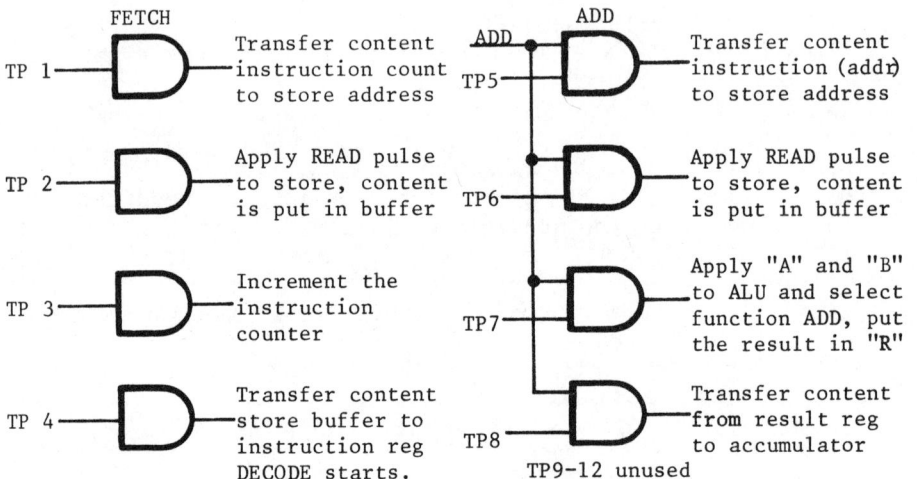

FETCH

TP 1 — Transfer content instruction count to store address

TP 2 — Apply READ pulse to store, content is put in buffer

TP 3 — Increment the instruction counter

TP 4 — Transfer content store buffer to instruction reg DECODE starts.

ADD

TP5 — Transfer content instruction (addr) to store address

TP6 — Apply READ pulse to store, content is put in buffer

TP7 — Apply "A" and "B" to ALU and select function ADD, put the result in "R"

TP8 — Transfer content from result reg to accumulator

TP9-12 unused

FIG. 4.6 COMMAND GENERATION

The ADD instruction steps are shown and, with time pulses 1-4 reserved for fetch, 5-8 are used for addition. A similar set of command generation gates would exist for each of the other instructions and it is easy to see how the precedence of the operate group would be arranged. Time pulses 5-7 could be used for clearing, complementing and incrementing, with shifts and rotations occurring during eight and nine, the rest being left for the tests which may adjust the program counter.

All the "store referencing" instructions could have the escape bit set to allow them to get at/to the full store. The use of this mechanism would take up some of the vacant time pulses.

To recap, the complete sequence for an instruction is:

Compute the instruction address.
Fetch the instruction.
Compute the effective address of any operands required.
Fetch the operands.
Perform the operation on them, producing a result.
Compute the effective address for storing the result.
Store the result.

5 Central Control Unit

5.1 MICRO-CONTROLLED MACHINES

It is apparent that by having fixed paths and hardwired gates performing the control sequences in the hardwired machine, we have limited its capabilities. For example, unless a path is added, data cannot get from the accumulator to the program counter except via store accesses. The machine is also limited to a fixed instruction set, hardwired in sets of gates, with control by the decoder and command generators. Some of these inherent disadvantages can be avoided by having a more general structure to the machine. This is called a *BUS HIGHWAY* structure, as every register is connected to a common "bus" of parallel wires and register transfers are accomplished by connecting the output and input of the desired registers to the bus. There are subsidiary busses on the arithmetic and logic unit inputs, since for many functions two input paths and one output path are required at the same time. Instead of gates throughout the machine (on various register inputs) to generate the command sequence, a bus highway system has a single set of gates for each register onto and off the main bus and a single output set of gates for the relevant registers to the subsidiary busses. These sets of gates are enabled by gate enable lines which are all taken to a *MICRO-INSTRUCTION* register, so that setting the appropriate bit in the micro-instruction register opens the desired gates.

Fields in the micro-instruction register also control the store, arithmetic and logical functions selected. A sequence of micro-instructions is held in a control store, which is a read only store (ROS), and these make up the complete instruction by performing the desired register transfers and function selects at the desired times. The sequence is normally "in line", but can be altered in the light of tests on bits by a field "sequence control" in the micro-instruction.

This type of machine is called a *MICRO-CONTROL* machine, sometimes referred to as a static microprogram machine. It has a permanently "wired" microprogram fixed in its read only store, so that changes can only be made by changing the read only store integrated circuits completely. Thus the advantage of altering instructions is only available to the manufacturer. It is possible to exchange this fixed read only store for one into which we can write occasionally, which must be protected by some kind of key-switch. A machine where we can write our own microprograms is called a microprogrammable machine or sometimes a dynamic microprogram machine. The store for microprograms is now a read mostly store, sometimes called a programmable read only store (PROS). It can have a very slow write cycle, as it is seldom written to, but as with the micro-control machine, the read cycle must be very fast.

Advantages of this sort of structure for a machine are: the elimination of some timing and control logic, as only one set of gates is used per register input or output; the ease of changing the instruction repertoire by changing the contents of the read only store and hence the micro-control sequence; the ease of implementing more complex instructions by adding more read only store and new algorithms, for instance, floating point instructions; the possibility of "emulation" of one machine by another, that is the complete replacement of the instruction set by that of another machine. Emulation can be done temporarily or even under instruction control, with both instruction sets held in the control store.

The disadvantages of this sort of structure are: the slower absolute speed of operation, determined by the read cycle time of the control store; the added cost of this store and its associated control, noting that it must be very fast; the requirement that the "key" for a microprogrammable machine must be securely held otherwise the instruction set can be tampered with and the machine "crashed". Many minicomputers used to be prepared to accept the disadvantages of fixed wiring to gain lower cost, but now, with advances in technology, control store can be made fast and cheap, and almost all computers use micro-control or microprogram structure for the flexibility it offers.

5.2 EXAMPLE OF A SIMPLE MICRO-CONTROL MACHINE

A simple machine has micro-instructions which contain fields of bits for gate control for registers, function control for the arithmetic and logic unit and the store, and sequence control. These fields could be coded up a little to avoid some illegal combinations, such as the input and output of a register being simultaneously open to the same bus, and to save space in the control store. A number of options in these fields are selected to give the micro-instruction.

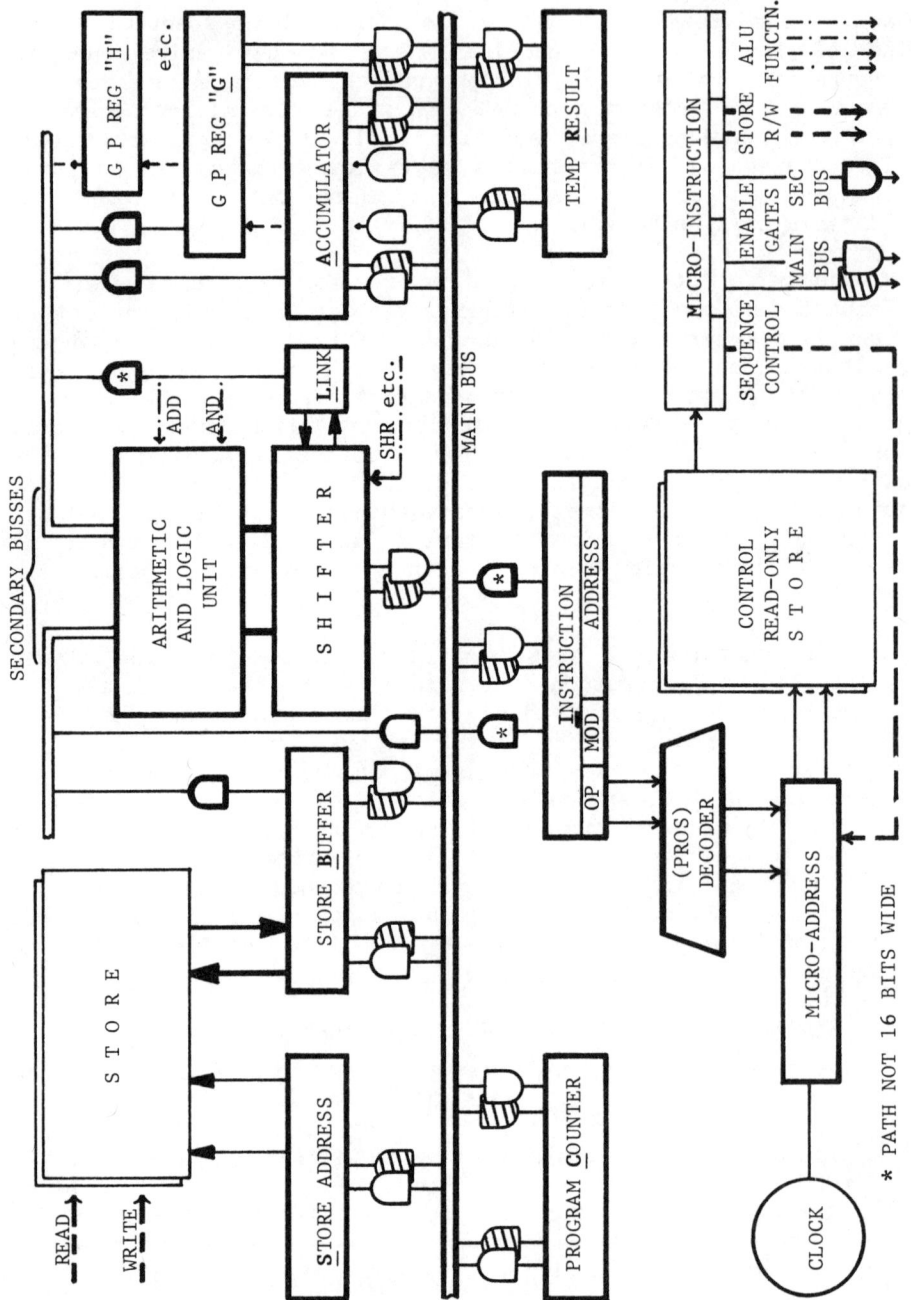

FIG. 5.1 *MICRO-CONTROL BUS HIGHWAY MACHINE*

To show this simply, mnemonics may be used for gate control of the registers "A", "B", "C", "I", "R", and "S" of the machine shown in Fig.5.1.

Ai open the input gates of the register nominated, A in this case.

Ao open the output gates of the register nominated, A in this case.

Ao.Bi do both specified operations at the same time.

Au open the output gates of the register specified to the secondary bus it is connected to.

Ui open the gates from the main bus to the secondary bus to the arithmetic and logic unit.

Uo open the output gates from the arithmetic and logic unit onto the main bus.

¬Ao open gates for the one's complement of the register specified onto the bus specified.

Function field options, much simplified, could be:

READ Read store contents of address specified in "S" and place them in "B".

WRITE Write contents of "B" into the location specified by the address in "S".

ADD Select the function ADD in the arithmetic and logic unit.

INC Select the function increment on the arithmetic unit by putting a carry into the least significant bit.

AND Select the function AND in the arithmetic and logic unit.

SHL Select left shift one place, output of arithmetic and logic unit.

SHR Select right shift one place, output of arithmetic and logic unit.

It could have the sequence control function options:

RES±N Reset the micro-operation sequence pointer (micro-address) to ±N microsteps from the current address.

SKO If the output of the arithmetic and logic unit is zero, add 1 to the micro-address in addition to the normal increment, thus skipping the next step in the micro-control sequence.

SKM If the most significant bit of the arithmetic and logic unit output is one, add 1 to the micro-address in addition to the normal increment, thus skipping the next step if the output is negative.

END Reset sequence pointer (micro-address) to zero at end of current step.

FIG. 5.2. MICRO-INSTRUCTION FIELDS

The same sequence of basic operations is needed to execute each instruction, and also the "fetch" sequence, as in the fixed wire machine, but the operations are now expressed as combinations of micro-orders and are held as bits in a ROS. To accomplish the fetch of an instruction, the current program counter is transferred to the store address register. The location is read by setting the READ line to the store and after the program counter has been incremented the instruction is transferred from the store buffer register to the instruction register. This sequence is shown in Fig.5.3a and takes only three steps, due to the logical structure of the machine. Only one adder is used and the incrementation of the program counter is done using it, as the store read progresses.

Once the instruction fetch has been completed, the instruction resides in the instruction register and the OP code is decoded. As mentioned earlier, another ROS contains the start address of the micro-control sequence for each instruction. If the ADD instruction OP code was found, 010 would be the input to the decoder and word 2 of the start address ROS would be got. This might be 50, as in Fig.5.3b, and the ADD instruction would be performed by the successive micro-instructions from 50 until the END bit was encountered. The BRAnch instruction is one of the simplest and fastest of instructions and its sequence is shown in Fig.5.3c.

0. $Co_{\wedge}Si_{\wedge}Bi$	50. $Si_{\wedge}Io**$	20. $Io_{\wedge}Ci_{\wedge}END**$
1. $Bu_{\wedge}Uo_{\wedge}Ci_{\wedge}INC_{\wedge}READ$	51. $READ$	
2. $Bo_{\wedge}Ii$	52. $Au_{\wedge}Bu_{\wedge}Uo_{\wedge}Ri_{\wedge}ADD$	** I 12 bit address
$DECODE$	53. $Ro_{\wedge}Ai_{\wedge}END$	field only
A) FETCH	B) ADD	C) BRANCH

FIG. 5.3 *SIMPLE MICRO-CONTROL SEQUENCES*

5.3   ADDRESSING MODES

As was mentioned in Chapter 1, any instruction can be fitted into the form:

RESULT = OPERAND {OPERATOR} OPERAND {NEXT INSTRUCTION}

There are five pieces of information required. The operator is normally specified by an OP code and the instructions are normally executed in sequence, so that the next instruction is contained in the location following the current instruction, unless a skip or branch operator is encountered which forces an alteration to the sequence. This leaves three required "fields" of information, which may be pointed to by addresses of store locations or may be implicit in the form of an instruction.

The machine structure discussed previously is termed a "single address" machine because only one address is specified in each instruction and the other two, the result and one operand, are implicitly the accumulator. It is perfectly possible to design a machine with an instruction format, such as:

ADD the content of location A to the content of location B, placing the result in the accumulator, or compare A with B and set flags to indicate greater than, equal to or less than. This is called a "double address" machine, as two addresses are specified.

A further possibility is:

ADD the content of location A to the content of location B and put the result in location C, which is a "triple address" machine.

The obvious disadvantage of these schemes is the increase in word length necessary to hold the extra addresses. The major advantages are a reduction in the number of instructions to perform a given program and the possibility of many accumulated result store locations, acting as accumulators. Machines often go part of the way towards this by having a normal single address structure for store accessing instructions, but also having general purpose registers which can be used as well as the accumulator as sources of operands and destinations for results. As there are only a few of these registers, two addresses can be fitted into the single address instruction word and so-called "register to register" instructions are made available. "Zero address" instructions have already been mentioned: in these all operands are implicit, for instance, rotates and shifts, or incrementing or complementing the accumulator.

The approach of using registers has some drawbacks: in particular it creates special cases when the registers are used up. If 16 registers are provided, some program is bound to require 17! As the cost of stores reduces, minicomputers are being extended to give full double address instructions, such as compare, or move from one location to another, as well as more traditional single address forms.

5.4   ADDRESS MODIFICATION

An instruction of the form shown in Fig.4.4 contains an operation code, a single bit address modification field and an address or operand field. Though address modification fields are normally larger than a single bit, the simple example will be used to show how various types of operand accessing (and hence address modification) work and how *EFFECTIVE ADDRESSES* are calculated. The single bit is used to specify that indirect addressing is required, as this is the method used to gain access to the whole 64K words of store.

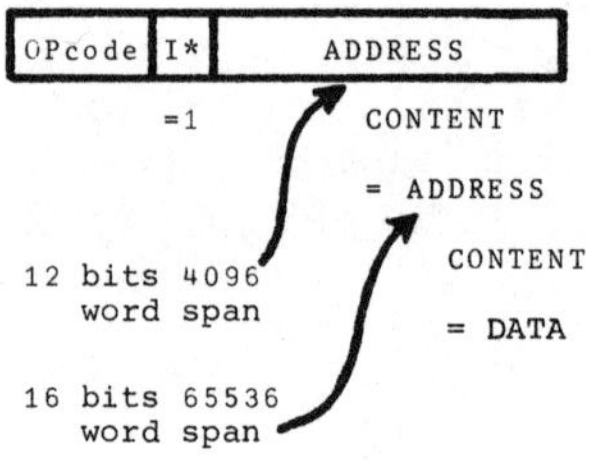

```
┌────────┬──┬──────────────┐
│ OPcode │I*│   ADDRESS    │          50.  Si∧Io**              ** 12 bit
└────────┴──┴──────────────┘                                       address
            =1         CONTENT          51.  Ui∧Io∧SKO∧READ *          field

                     = ADDRESS          52.  RES+3                 *  1 bit
                                                                     indirect
   12 bits 4096          CONTENT        53.  Au∧Bu∧Uo∧Ri∧ADD           field
   word span
                         = DATA         54.  Ro∧Ai∧END

   16 bits 65536                        55.  Bo∧Si·
   word span
                                        56.  READ

                                        57.  RES-4

A) INDIRECT ADDRESSING                  B) MICRO-CONTROL SEQUENCE
```

FIG. 5.4 INDIRECT ADDRESSING AND ADD SEQUENCE

When the "I" bit is zero direct addressing is indicated and one of 4096 words can be specified in the address field. When the "I" bit is set to a one, it indicates that the operand of the current instruction is not held at the address given in the instruction, but that it is contained in the location specified by treating those contents as an address, as shown in Fig.5.4. For example, ADD I 230 does not add the contents of location 230 (say 12072) to the accumulator: as indirect addressing is specified, it takes those contents (12072), treats them as an address and hence actually performs the instruction ADD the contents of location 12072 (say 50). Thus the address is modified to give access to the entire store. Branching in a program may also be indirect so that both instructions and data can be accessed anywhere in the store. If a field of bits is available for address modification, then the following types would be considered:

IMMEDIATE ADDRESSING: The required operand is not addressed at all, as it is either implicit (zero address) or else is actually held in the instruction in the address field instead of an address.

DIRECT ADDRESSING: The address field of the instruction is the required address. This is often referred to as zero page addressing, as a 64K word store could be considered as a set of 16 "pages" of 4096 words each. Direct addressing only reaches the bottom page.

RELATIVE ADDRESSING: The address field of the instruction is taken relative to the start of the "page" which contains the instruction. In practice, this means the least significant twelve bits of the effective address are the address field of the instruction and the most significant four bits are the most significant four bits of the program counter.

PROGRAM COUNTER RELATIVE: The address field of the instruction is taken as an offset relative to the program counter, thus allowing a range of -2048 to +2047 around the current instruction. The twelve bit field has the most significant bit propogated up to the sixteenth bit, giving a positive or negative sixteen bit offset to be added to the program counter to give the effective address.

INDIRECT ADDRESSING: As described in the simple example, the content of the location specified in the address field of the instruction is taken as the effective address. Another method is to have the "indirect" bit as the most significant bit of every word: any word with its most significant bit set to one, if accessed as an address, implies that a further indirection is to take place. This has one drawback, that a closed loop can occur by an indirect, indirect, giving the address of the first location.

INDEXED ADDRESSING: A similar effect to indirection can be obtained by adding the address field of the instruction to the contents of a register to compute the effective address. Such a register is called an *INDEX* register, but may also be usable as a general purpose accumulator. If an array is stored, then elements of it can be addressed with the same instruction simply by changing the content of the index register. Index addressing can coexist with indirect addressing: pre-indexing or post-indexing will then have to be selected, depending on whether the index is done before the indirection or the indirection done before the index. The inclusion of such features as indexing is obviously eased by micro-control structures, as only ROS changes are involved. An example of the changed micro-control sequence for indirect ADD is in Fig.5.4.

Various address modification methods are included in modern minicomputers, but they obviously require some bits in the instruction word, so a single sixteen bit word may be insufficient, particularly for double address type instructions. A variable length of instruction is often encountered, some being a single word and some two words long, to give the extensions to addresses that are desirable.

5.5 GENERAL PURPOSE REGISTERS

General purpose registers are included to allow instructions to be performed without using store locations for intermediate results. They thus double as accumulators and index registers. They are also used to hold counts for multiple shift instructions and for instructions such as multiply. The multiply instruction will be used as an example of these features, Fig.5.5 showing its micro-instruction sequence, with the instruction definition being:

Multiply the contents of location "n" by the contents of the accumulator (1) producing a double length result in the accumulator (1) and general purpose register (2). Two general purpose registers are used as well as a link; with the previous mnemonic convention the registers are labelled "G" and "H" and the link is labelled "L".

100. $Io_\wedge Si_\wedge Lc$	Address field 'n' to store, clear link.
101. $Ao_\wedge Gi_\wedge READ$	Accumulator to multiplier reg (use "G").
102. $Ri_\wedge CONST[-15]$	Constant minus 15 from ALU to temporary.
103. $Ro_\wedge Hi$	Count returned from temporary to "H".
104. $Gu_\wedge Uo_\wedge Ri_\wedge SHR$	Test bit to link, calculated bit saved.
105. $Ro_\wedge Gi$	Shifted multiplier held for next cycle.
106. $Lu_\wedge SKO_\wedge Ao_\wedge Ri$	See if test bit 0 or 1, if 0 then no add.
107. $Au_\wedge Bu_\wedge Uo_\wedge Ri_\wedge ADD$	If "1", add multiplicand to current sum.
108. $Ru_\wedge Uo_\wedge Ai_\wedge SHR$	Shift & save sum, new answer bit to link.
109. $Hu_\wedge Ri_\wedge INC_\wedge SKO_\wedge Uo$	Increment cycle counter, finished if 0.
110. $RES-7$	Repeat whole cycle for next test bit.
111. $Gu_\wedge Uo_\wedge Hi_\wedge SHR_\wedge END$	DONE! leave 32 bit result in A and H.

FIG. 5.5 *UNSIGNED MULTIPLICATION MICRO-CONTROL*

5.6 INTERPRETIVE MACHINES

A fourth type of machine can be produced, which is called either a soft machine or an interpretive machine. Its basic feature is that it has no instruction set as such, at the level considered previously, but only a micro-instruction set. This means that it does not have instructions at the level of ADD or MULTIPLY, etc. but only micro-instructions, such as have been described, for opening gates, selecting functions and controlling timing. This might seem to be a disadvantage, but it can produce a much better general purpose "target" machine for use with high-level languages.

A soft machine is used by writing an interpretive program in micro-code to produce a "target" machine, which is most suited to the high-level language in which the applications programs are to be written. This is done for all languages which are to be used and when a given interpreter is loaded, the machine becomes a most efficient "COBOL machine", "ALGOL machine" or "FORTRAN 4 machine".

Because there is no limitation to a given instruction set having certain arithmetic and logical functions, the full range of capabilities of the hardware is available and a more efficient machine for a particular purpose may result. For example, the usual general purpose minicomputer is very restricted in string-handling operations, not because its basic hardware is incapable of these operations, but because the manufacturers and designers thought it more viable to include other instructions in the "set". Thus a soft machine has an interpreter for a target machine for each language, which is the equivalent of the instruction set, and the "compilers" translate the high-level language program into the operations of the chosen target machine to produce running programs. The target machine is designed mainly from the high-level language, choosing those operations which will make for efficient running and coding this target up in micro-instructions. The whole system and its software is then a simple efficient APL, COBOL or ALGOL machine.

The microprograms of a dynamic microprogram machine and the interpreters of a soft machine are referred to as FIRMWARE. With a micro-control machine the firmware is restricted to those instructions and system functions which will not need changing. Modern machines include the basic instruction set and complex instructions, floating point operations, interrupt handling, message passing and parts of paging operations in their firmware.

Four types of machine structure have been identified for control units:

HARDWIRED machine, which has an INSTRUCTION REGISTER and an INSTRUCTION SET and has its control sequences fixed, wired into it in the form of command generators.

MICRO-CONTROL machine, which has an INSTRUCTION REGISTER and a MICRO-INSTRUCTION REGISTER, with INSTRUCTION and MICRO-INSTRUCTION SETS. It has its control sequences held in a fixed read only store, but they can be changed if the fixed store is changed.

MICROPROGRAMMABLE machine, which has everything as for a micro-control machine, but the control sequences can be altered by the user, via a programmable read only store or writable control store.

INTERPRETIVE machine, which has only a MICRO-INSTRUCTION REGISTER and a MICRO-INSTRUCTION SET and no fixed instructions at any other level than the basic control steps.

If the basic instruction set of the machine is altered, then the guarantees and service contracts with the manufacturer are often invalidated. A second difficulty is that a very high degree of machine knowledge is required for successful microprogram writing. The average problem-solving programmer will experience difficulty producing firmware at such a detailed level. It is desirable, when writing problem-solving programs, to program in as high a level of language as possible to permit accurate specification of the problem and solution. However, to produce microprograms a very detailed approach is essential, far more akin to logic design than to high-level language problem solving.

5.7 MACHINE STATUS AND INPUT-OUTPUT

Many flags in the machine are concerned with its "status". Such flags are normally set or cleared as the result of an instruction or following the occurrence of some internal or external condition. It may be necessary to clear indications of error conditions or to set up a particular status for a program, hence it is common practice to group many of these flags together to form a register. This approach simplifies the testing and altering of machine status because it does not require extra instructions. The same instructions which are used to test and alter any other register can be used with the status register.

Some flags which may be found in a status register are:

comparison bits signifying "less than", "greater than" or "equal to" as the result of an instruction;

bits indicating the state in which the machine is running (problem state, system state, wait state);

substate indication, e.g. pre- or post-indexing;

overflow and overrange conditions;

a carry or link;

interrupt conditions, possibly multi-level, enabled or disabled as described in Chapters 6 and 7;

internal error conditions (described in Chapters 9 and 10) such as illegal instruction, protected store violation or store parity error.

Problems can be caused by this very simple approach if more than one program resides in the machine as each may require different status settings. The ability to alter status may be reserved for some priviledged state or program (probably the operating system); extra bits of the status register are used to show in which state the machine is running. Changes are then only made in an orderly fashion but ordinary programs can still interrogate the status register.

To implement very simple input-output, we could add a register to the bus as shown in Fig.6.1. It is controlled by a "flag". If the flag is set, then some action is required, and if not, then the peripheral is not busy. The output of a character involves putting the character into the peripheral register (P) and setting the flag to "1". The device will, on this indication, take the character and output it, and when the peripheral has dealt with the character, it sets the flag back to "0". If input were required instead, then the flag would be set by the peripheral and the machine would look at the flag to see if it were a "1" and transfer the content of the "P" register into store if it were. This could be handled by changing the fetch sequence of control to check if the flag is set for input. This is the method used for interrupts and is described in Chapter 7, with sample microcode shown in Fig.7.8.

6 Simple Input-Output and Peripherals

6.1 PROGRAMMED INPUT-OUTPUT

A simple input-output arrangement is shown in Fig.6.1. A single register has inputs from the computer and also from a set of switches: it has its outputs connected to the computer and also to a set of lamps (or light-emitting diodes). To read in the content of the set of switches, the gates for the switches are enabled, followed by the clock. The register then contains the number (bit pattern) from the switches. For output, the bit pattern to be output is transferred to the register via the set of gates from the computer and the clock is pulsed. The pattern appears on the lamps. This can obviously be done by a program. If more than one device is to be serviced, then the machine will need codes to decide with which device the input or output is concerned.

Transfers are started by an XIO instruction which specifies the device, and a function. Typical functions are:

READ the contents of the peripheral register, into the accumulator.

WRITE the contents of the accumulator to the peripheral register.

SKIP the next instruction if the flag for the device specified is set.

CLEAR the device flag and its peripheral register.

A sequence of instructions to output to a simple printer would include clearing the device flag, writing the character to the peripheral register and then testing for completion using the "skip if flag set" function. This sequence would be repeated for every character printed. As most peripherals are very slow in computer terms (e.g. switching by humans would take a few seconds, while the computer would do many million operations in this time), it is wasteful to do nothing while waiting for a peripheral to finish an action. Thus for a device such as a card reader, a command to read the next card is given and the normal program continues, with a look every so often at a flag to see if the character is in the register yet. This is called *POLLING* the flag. It is obviously inconvenient to have to perform polling for many peripherals within a program unless the program is only performing input-output (as in a peripheral processor). The procedure is often moved into hardware and called an *INTERRUPT*.

Transfers are started by the program as before (by XIO instruction) and the hardware checks the flags for all devices before every instruction to see if any have changed. If a flag has changed, an interrupt is generated. This forces the program counter (the pointer to the current instruction in the program) to be stored and forces a jump to a standard location for service. Active registers will also have to be stored, and unless a stack method is used, re-entrant programming will not be possible.

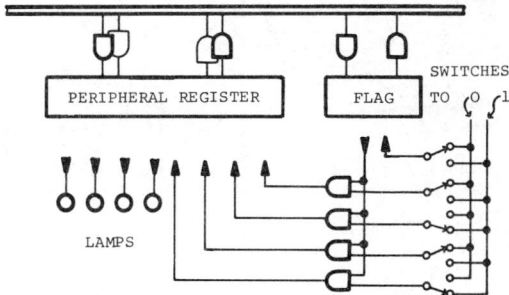

FIG. 6.1 *SIMPLE INPUT-OUTPUT*

The simplest interrupt method uses a single location for all interrupts and a series of checks then determines which flag caused the interrupt. This is a single level non-priority interrupt scheme and is sometimes called a *SKIP-CHAIN*, as the method of checking is often to have instructions of the form: "skip if flag set". The only priority it provides is the order of checking the flags, which can be altered by the program in the light of its needs. The interrupts must be disabled while the interrupt is in progress to ensure that continuity is not lost. This system is cheap, but wasteful of time. It is sufficient for the moment for slow peripherals: more complex systems are discussed further on.

6.2 KEYBOARDS

The most common peripheral for input from humans to machines is a keyboard. Like a typewriter keyboard, but with the ability to generate seven bit codes for each key depressed, rather than a mechanical movement, it permits a typist to input program, text or control commands rapidly. The code produced is normally ASC11, although there are other codes. There are many switching methods to provide the signal which is used to select the code for sending into the computer.

"Reed" switches incorporate two plated reeds, cantilevered from each end of a sealed glass tube: the proximity of a magnet causes them to pull together and contact. They are usually more reliable than simple switches. Other techniques use capacitive coupling, magnetic effects, including the "Hall" effect, and elastomeric conductors to detect the key depression. The data produced (7 bits) normally has an eighth bit added as a check and is then sent to the computer serially, bit by bit, so that a keyboard can be remotely connected using only two wires. Start and stop bits surround the code so that the hardware knows when to accept a character.

5x7 DOT MATRIX

FIG. 6.2 PRINTING COMPUTER TERMINAL

Rollover protection is normally provided to prevent a character being produced wrongly if more than one key is depressed. There is little point in connecting a keyboard at any transmission speed higher than 30 characters per second, as no typist could exceed this, but for hardware similarity (with a printer, say), a higher speed may be used.

6.3 PRINTERS

The most important source of permanent computer output is a printer. There are three basic mechanisms in a printer: to move the paper vertically; to locate the printing mechanism horizontally; finally to produce the printed character. The differing methods used to solve these problems, give rise to criteria of types of printers: SERIAL or LINE; IMPACT or NON-IMPACT; CHARACTER or MATRIX.

All printers use basically similar mechanisms to move the paper vertically to the correct line. An electric motor and control, arranged so that it moves either in very small steps (1/48") or a complete one line movement at a time, drives either a "pinched roller", similar to that in a typewriter, or a "sprocket" feed. The sprocket drives the paper by meshing with holes previously punched every half inch down its sides. It normally gives a more accurate drive, as the paper can not slip, and is used in all high speed printers. It is normal to control a sprocket feed using whole line movements by a carriage control tape. A loop of paper has holes punched in it, corresponding to each line and the start of a page. Light shining through the holes onto detectors controls the movement. The serial/line distinction classifies printers by the amount of print produced at one time and hence by horizontal positioning method. A serial printer prints one character at a time and then moves the printing mechanism on to the next position. A "line" printer accumulates the character codes for a whole line in a buffer register and then prints the whole line. This implies that there is no movement of the whole printing mechanism, but that there is some mechanism for each and every print position.

To distinguish the mechanical method of character impression, the impact/non-impact criteria is used. An impact printer makes physical contact between the typeface and the paper, with some force, using an inked or carbon ribbon so that the character appears. A non-impact printer uses an electrostatic or thermal method which requires no force to produce type. Non-impact printers are generally quieter and more reliable than the impact types. Special paper is normally required for the non-impact types, sometimes with a chemical coating which turns black if heated by a thermal print head.

The way in which the outline of the character is formed is distinguished by character or matrix. The characters of the "character" type are fully formed in mirror image on a drum, wheel, "golfball" or "train". This type gives superior character quality (this book was printed using one!), but can only be used by impact printing. All other forms use a matrix of tiny dots to build up a character. This type of printer is often simpler to drive, but the characters lack quality: even a matrix of 9x7 dots is easily noticed when compared with character printing.

The normal fast printer is an impact, line, character printer and is sketched in Fig.6.3. The characters are formed in mirror image on "slugs" which form a "train", though they could be connected to a chain. The train is driven round at high speed by a motor and markers on the drive indicate where particular characters occur. An inked ribbon is placed between the train of characters and the paper, and this also is advanced by a motor after a line is printed. Each print position (there are normally between 72 and 160, with 80 and 132 being international standards) has a solenoid operated hammer mounted behind the paper. Thus when the character code held in the buffer matches the code for the character slug, in the same position, the hammer is driven and the paper and ribbon hit the character slug in the train, printing the character. This action goes on for all characters in the buffer at about the same time as they appear in front of the hammers. The line appears to be printed at one instant hence the name.

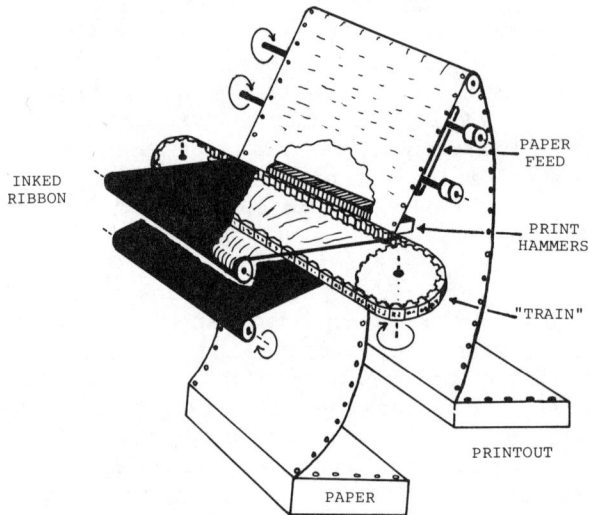

FIG. 6.3 LINE PRINTER {TRAIN}

Drums with the characters on them, rotated around a horizontal axis, used to be used but the human eye is far more sensitive to vertical misalignment caused by striking a character too early on a drum than it is to the horizontal misalignment caused by striking a character on a train a little early or late. This is easily seen by looking at this page. There are unequal spaces between words on different lines which pass unnoticed, whereas a vertical discrepancy of the same size is immediately obvious.

Serial printers all have some method of moving the single print head along a track, using a motor to position it for the next character to be printed. At the end of a line a "carriage return" control character is sent, which restores the head to the start of the line. Serial printers have a far greater variety of print generation methods: some of these are shown in Fig.6.4. Impact printers use a small wheel or a "golfball" with a mirror image character set and a ribbon and hammer as for a line printer. An impact matrix technique exists where a line of solenoid-driven pins are driven behind a ribbon onto the paper. Selecting the correct pins creates the character outline. For non-impact printing the range of techniques is wide; it includes producing charged droplets of ink in the form of a spray to be deflected electrostatically to draw the character, or charging up the paper in patterns of dots (also electrostatically) and then sprinkling carbon dust over the paper to stick where it is attracted. This is similar to the method of xerographic copying. A recent development of this gives very high speed printing by using an indirect, whole-page generation technique. A light-sensitive photo-conductor (mounted on a rotating drum) is charged, and then exposed to characters formed by modulating a "laser" light beam. The drum is rotated past a toner application station where black powder adheres in the dot pattern formed by the light. The drum rotates further to pass a transfer station where the whole-page of powder patterns is transferred to ordinary paper prior to being baked on by heated rollers.

Perhaps the simplest and most attractive of the non-impact matrix printers is the thermal printer. The thermal machine uses solid state technology to produce a matrix of small dot resistors, which heat the paper in the patterns for the character required. With specially coated paper this forms the printed character.

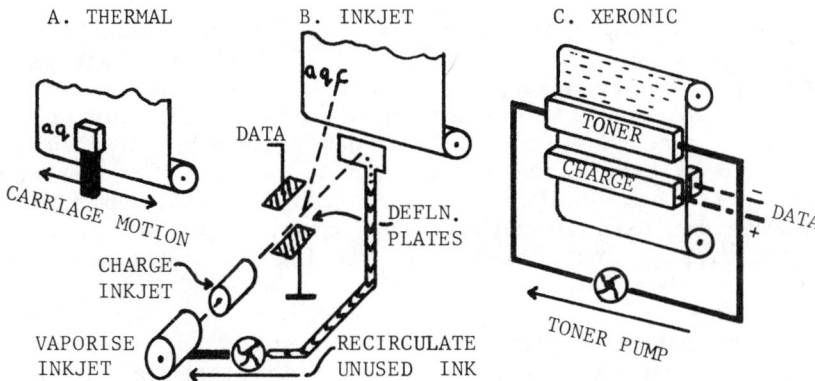

FIG. 6.4 *NON-IMPACT PRINT MECHANISMS*

Operating speed is measured either in characters per second (cps) for serial printers or in lines per minute (lpm) for line printers. Printers are made ranging from 30 cps thermal printers with keyboards acting as computer terminals (Fig.6.2), through the standard 1000 lpm impact line printer used on many computers, to 20,000 lpm super speed laser printers.

6.4   VISUAL DISPLAYS

Visual displays produce soft copy, which can be overwritten or erased, so that the screen can be used to display more information. A classification of displays divides them into *ALPHANUMERIC*, able to display numerals, letters and certain punctuation and other symbols, or *GRAPHIC*, able to display diagrams. Except for "X-Y" only displays, graphic units always include an alphanumeric capability. Character displays can be made using a dot matrix of light emitting diodes, or a gas discharge tube, but these are normally limited to a few characters.

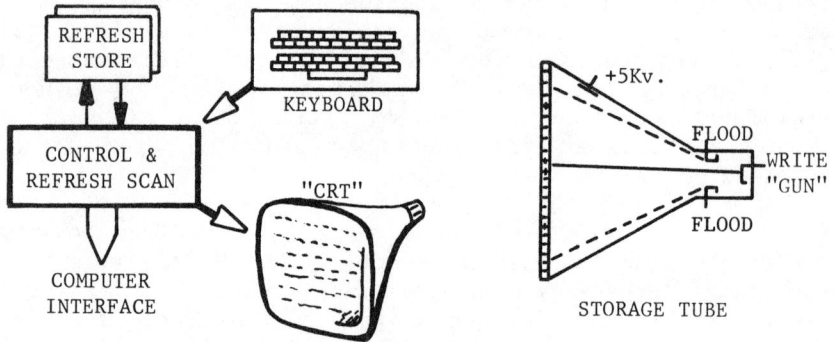

FIG. 6.5 *VISUAL DISPLAY UNITS*

The standard displays are "cathode ray" tubes, similar to those used in televisions, and until a flat screen display is perfected, they are likely to remain in a dominant position in the market. Alphanumeric displays have up to 40 lines of up to 80 characters per line on the screen. Graphic displays are categorised by the number of addressable points on the screen. A common format has 750,000 individually addressable points. The two mechanisms used in cathode ray tubes, shown in Fig.6.5, to form the display and hold it for viewing are refreshed screens and storage tubes.

Refreshed screen display: Data for display on the screen is transmitted from the computer to a buffer store in the display unit. The data, held in coded form, is translated into character form by character generation logic and is put up to the screen in the form of a scanned electron beam. A phosphor coating on the inside of the screen glows when hit by the electron beam and the glow persists for a short time. If the whole pattern is repeated often enough, approximately fifty times a second, the display appears fixed and the characters (and graphics) are viewed with ease. If a sufficiently high refresh rate is not maintained, then flickering of the picture is observed. Phosphors have a persistance (to 10%) which is typically 50ms. to nearly a second for computer terminals. Practical limits are set on the buffer size and on the writing speed, or speed of movement of the electron beam, as it is deflected by electromagnet or electrostatic charge, so a limit is set on the complexity of a display. As the data is held in a buffer store, partial erasure and partial updating are possible.

If a special phosphor coating is used, with a clever arrangement of electron beams, data can be stored actually on the face of the screen. This system has no flicker and no limit to the amount of data on the screen until the whole screen is over-written. The main disadvantage is that partial erase is not possible, only a complete erasure of the screen, taking about 1/2 second.

The special phosphor stays dark if it is charged negatively and lights up if it is charged positively. A slow electron beam (flood) covers the screen and as an electron (-ve charge) approaches the unlit screen (-ve charge), it is repelled, so the charge remains negative and the screen unlit. A narrow highspeed electron beam is used to write onto the screen, the velocity of the electrons overcoming the force of repulsion. As an electron from the beam hits the screen, it dislodges many other electrons (like billiard balls) and leaves a net positive charge, which glows. The hit area remains positively charged under the flood action, as the positive area attracts electrons from the flood beam and accelerates them to hit the screen at speed, dislodging electrons. Erasing the screen is performed by flooding the screen with high speed electrons, to turn it all positive, and then removing the flood, so that it all returns to its quiescent negative state.

6.5   CARD READERS AND PUNCHES

Non-erasable, machine-readable hard copy is almost exclusively the preserve of punched cards and paper tape. Standard cards have 80 columns of 12 hole positions each, but each character only has 3 or less holes punched. There is often blank space on a card as it normally represents one line of program or data. The access to cards is sequential but the characters can be read either in the "slow" direction (12 bits at a time), or sideways 80 bits at a time over the 12 columns. A buffer store is required for the latter method, as the characters must be reassembled. Reading is accomplished using photo-electric sensors, detecting light shining through the holes. Punching the holes in the cards is, as might be expected, a rather crude process, with sharp, oblong knives being pushed by electro-magnetic solenoids. The problems with card feeding, and the speed of movement of the knives, limit punch speeds to 400 cards per minute, though cards may be read at around 1000 cards a minute.

A new development has been the 96 column card. Half the size of the standard card, and using coding more akin to paper tape, they are used in small business machines. Three rows of 32 eight bit characters, using circular holes, denote the characters. All the card media are loosing popularity, as the re-usable media gain in reliability and convenience.

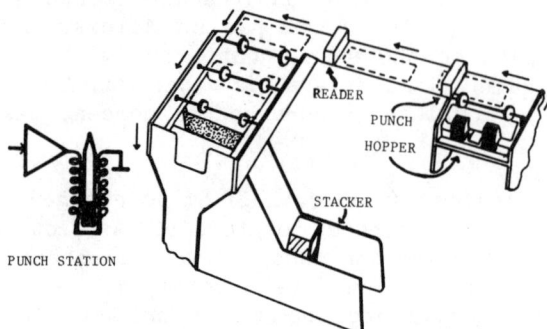

FIG. 6.6 *COMBINED CARD READER AND PUNCH*

Paper tape, a continuous strip of 1" wide paper, has up to eight holes punched across it to give the standard ASCII code. A smaller "sprocket" hole is used to feed the tape, and with its own photo-sensor acts as a strobe, locating the centre of the punched character. The mechanisms are similar to those for cards, but much cheaper, and with speeds from 100-1000 characters per second, are very popular as mini- and microcomputer peripherals, despite the problem of handling large rolls of tape.

7 Complex Input-Output

7.1 AUTONOMOUS INPUT-OUTPUT

Input and output operations could be performed in the simple fashion described in the previous chapter, but there are a number of reasons for preferring autonomy between the central processor and any input-output.

INFORMATION FLOW-RATE DIFFERENCE: whilst a central processor performs transfers to and from the store at a rate of 8-100 bits per microsecond, input-output devices seldom reach one bit per microsecond and are normally in the range 1-300 bits per millisecond.

QUANTUM DIFFERENCE: it is normal to store information in words in the computer store, but devices are more concerned with characters, or even bits for serial data transmission or recording.

DEVICE CONFLICT AND SYNCHRONISATION: at any time, two or more devices may require service, having completed an operation or encountered an error condition. The devices can only transfer data to/from the store at times when the store is ready and so some form of synchronisation must take place.

DEVICE CONNECTION: with the simple system every device has to be connected to the central control unit, and the additional wire lengths and their loading requirements will slow down the operation of data transfers.

An added advantage of autonomous I-0 is the versatility it affords, by removing routine housekeeping problems from the complex central control unit and solving them in a simple I-0 controller, leaving the central control unit free to perform its primary functions.

7.2 DATA CHANNELS

Input and output operations are performed by a controller, which is called a "channel". There are various types of channels, the division into *SELECTOR* and *MULTIPLEXOR* channels arising from whether they select only one device for a given transfer or multiplex many parallel transfers at one time. A simple example of a selector channel will be described first.

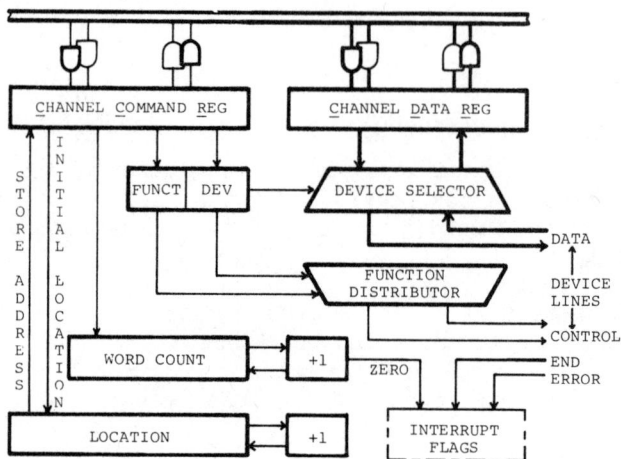

FIG. 7.1 SELECTOR CHANNEL LOGIC

Channel command words, of the form shown below, are stored in the main store. When I-O is commenced, the first of these is sent to the channel and it instructs the channel to perform a particular set of operations with a given device. Only one device at a time may transfer data through the selector channel. The channel commands are of the form:

FUNCTION {DEVICE} COUNT {LOCATION} FLAGS

The channel, on receiving a command, decodes the device field and selects the required peripheral. The word count (stored as minus the desired number) and the initial location are put in registers in the channel. For input, characters are read in from the device and assembled into a word. The channel then stores this word in the location specified and increments the location and count registers. It then assembles the next word and so on until the count is zero (by incrementing the negative count up until zero is reached) or an error flag is set, when an interrupt is generated and the computer has to take some action.

Thus a channel performs a transfer of a large "block" of data independently of the central processor. This "block transfer" facility is also more logical for a programmer as data seldom consists of single characters, but normally contains data elements or "records" which are quite long are logically connected and should be handled as a single entity. The channel commands can be chained together, so the channel can gather and scatter data from and to various parts of the store and input and output can be interleaved. It solves the synchronisation problems by assembling complete words at the device speed, then causing a *HESITATION* or cycle stealing operation, during which the processor is held up for the cycle required by the channel to get (or put) a word from (or to) the store. When using programmed I-0, the central processor has all data passing through it, to the store. A channel just takes the form of another competing processor for the store. As there are many fewer store accesses and instructions for I-0, the central processor will perform better, but it will be given the lowest priority for store access, as it can always wait, and some of the devices (such as a disc) can not. This is a single port store access scheme. Even with this improvement processor performance is degraded when input and output occur as cycles are "stolen".

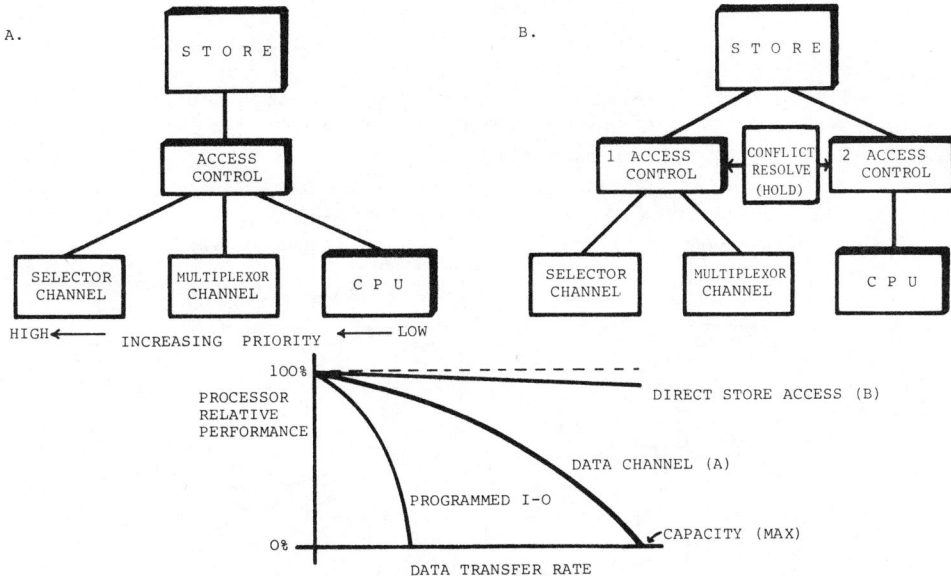

FIG. 7.2 DATA CHANNEL AND D.S.A. INPUT-OUTPUT

A multiplexor channel on the other hand is designed for connecting a large number of slow devices (e.g. terminals) to the computer and can accept characters at random from any device, assembling them up into words. It takes longer to input the word because the multiplexor channel has to fetch the location and counter for this device from store by stealing cycles, increment them and return them again by stealing cycles before being able to store the data word in the location specified. Thus, instead of stealing a single cycle, it steals a number of cycles (3-5) for each word input to, or output from, store. It makes up for this lack of efficiency by taking the whole load of input and output for many terminals from the central processor.

7.3   DIRECT STORE ACCESS

This is a term which many manufacturers misuse, as it should only be used to describe a system with more than a single access port to the store. Thus, the processor has its own store access control and all input and output goes via another; the processor should only be affected slightly by the I-0, as no cycle stealing is involved. Some logic is required to settle any conflicts (on a priority basis), should both mechanisms desire access to the same part of store at the same time, but apart from this, there should be no degradation of processor performance. The DSA system has its own store address and store buffer (data) registers, as well as those registers found in an ordinary channel.

As can be seen, there is a maximum data transfer rate that the computer can take. There will also be similar maxima for each channel. This is called the "capacity" of the channel and is expressed in bits per second (bps), or bytes or words per sec. In a single port store access system the processor "stalls" when the total input-output transfer rate reaches the capacity of the store, as all cycles are being stolen for I-0.

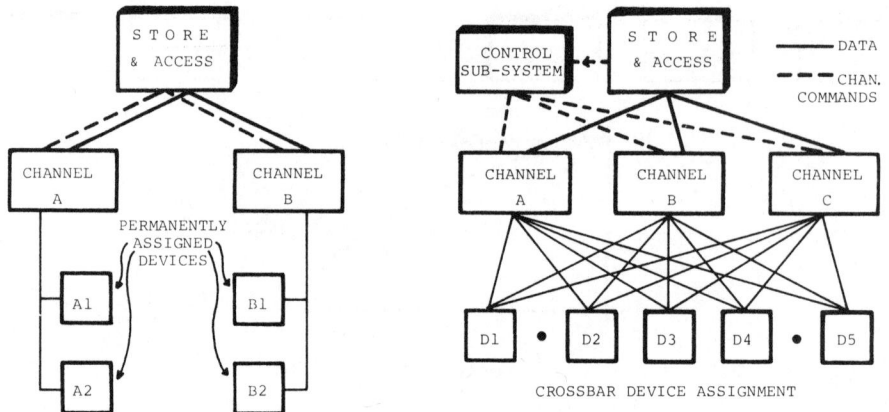

FIG. 7.3 AUTONOMOUS I/O DEVICE ASSIGNMENT

A further consideration when channels or direct store access mechanisms are used is the way in which devices are connected to the channels. If, as in many small computers, only a single data channel is used, there is no problem, as all the devices requiring autonomous I-0 will be connected to it. High data

throughput or device conflicts might dictate the use of more than
one channel. Devices would have to be allocated to each channel.
This *PERMANENT* device assignment is simple and easy to implement,
but suffers from the drawback that a selector channel can only
keep one device active at an instant. Even if the best possible
allocation is made at program run-time, it is likely that
conflicts will occur, with two devices (say A1 and A2 in Fig.7.3)
being required at the same time. If the devices were on separate
channels both could be active all the time, with an obvious
improvement in throughput.

"Crossbar" assignment overcomes this problem, at the expense of
added hardware complexity. Every device is connected to every
channel. During program execution, the "control sub-system" takes
channel commands from the main store and allocates them to the
next free channel. (In the permanent system, each channel gets
its own channel commands directly.) The channel then selects the
device and sets flags for itself and the device, to show busy
status, so that other attempts will not be made to gain access to
them. On completion of the channnel command, the control sub-
system will allocate any further commands for the device to the
channel, otherwise both the channel and the device are released
to the "free pool", until required again. This system, shown as
Fig.7.3b, is of particular use in real-time and time sharing
systems running many programs simultaneously, in which any
combination of circumstances may upset any previously defined
arrangement. Note that with all channel arrangements the number
of interrupts and the processor I-O handling load are drastically
reduced.

7.4   SURFACE MAGNETIC RECORDING PRINCIPLES

In any surface magnetic recording system, such as magnetic tape,
cassette, or disc, the basic principles are the same. A base
material is coated with a magnetisable material, normally Gamma
Fe_2O_3. This surface is moved past a read-write head, either in
contact (tape systems), or with a minute air gap, as small as 0.1
micrometres, for disc systems. The read-write head is simply a
coil of wire, forming an electro-magnet. If an electric current
is passed through a coil, a magnetic field is induced. This field
can be concentrated, to act over a small area, by inserting a
ring of a "soft" magnetic material. (A soft magnetic material
does not retain any permanent magnetisation; typical materials
used are "ferroxcube" and "mumetal" alloys.) A small air gap is
left in the ring and the majority of the magnetic field induced
by the coil is concentrated to act only across the gap. If the
gap is placed close to the magnetisable surface of the tape or
disc, the concentrated magnetic field induces the formation of
small magnetised areas on the surface. These "magnets" will be

formed in one direction or the other depending on the direction of the current through the coil. Thus two states are available for recording zeros and ones, as patterns of magnetic domains in the surface layer.

To read a tape or disc, the previously recorded surface pattern is moved past the head, but instead of driving a current through the coil, it is connected to a sense amplifier. As the surface is moved past the head, each little magnet of the pattern induces a magnetic field in the head, and changes produce a small current in the coil. The change of flux, when the magnetisation switches from one direction to the other, is a detectable event and it appears as a small voltage pulse in the coil. This is amplified by the sense amplifier and is restored to normal logic levels.

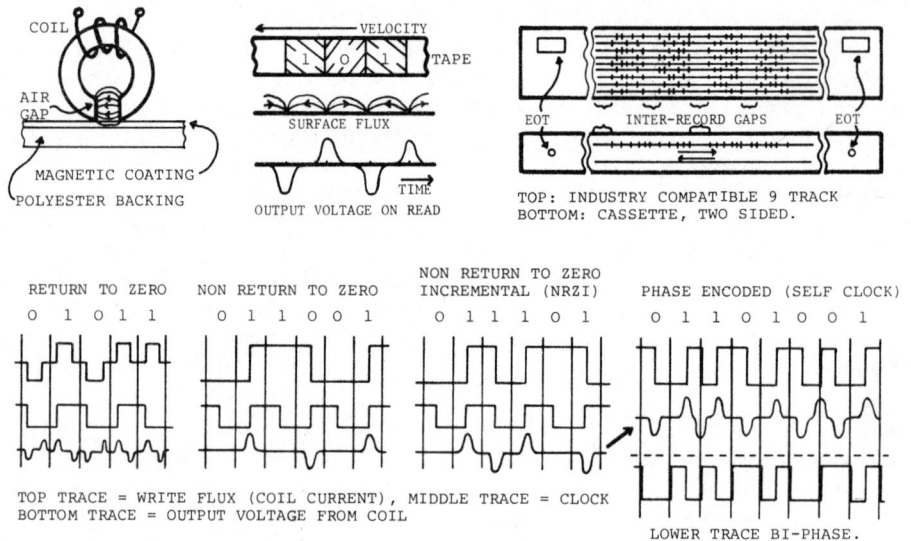

TOP: INDUSTRY COMPATIBLE 9 TRACK
BOTTOM: CASSETTE, TWO SIDED.

TOP TRACE = WRITE FLUX (COIL CURRENT), MIDDLE TRACE = CLOCK
BOTTOM TRACE = OUTPUT VOLTAGE FROM COIL

LOWER TRACE BI-PHASE.

FIG. 7.4 SURFACE MAGNETIC RECORDING PRINCIPLES

There are many ways of encoding the data on the tape, using combinations of the three possible states in which the tape may exist. The states are unrecorded (blank or erased), recorded with magnetisation in the zero direction, or recorded with magnetisation in the one direction.

RETURN TO ZERO: In a return to zero system all three states are used, with "0" and "1" being assigned unique directions of magnetisation, and the pulses for this data being separated by periods when no current flows in the coil and no magnetisation is recorded. Pre-erasing the tape to remove any prior recording is essential, before any new information can be written, to leave the blank areas. A sketch of the waveforms for this scheme and the others described is shown in Fig.7.4. A clock is not strictly necessary to read the data, as an erased portion of tape appears between each magnetic "cell" (which represents a single bit). The disadvantages of this system, pre-erasing requiring an extra write head, and the low packing density due to the blank spaces on the tape, suggest that a method of recording using only the magnetised directions without returning to zero could be preferable.

NON-RETURN TO ZERO: In the NRZ systems the magnetic coating of the tape or disc is always magnetised in one direction or the other. In the simplest NRZ scheme, the flux changes only with a change in the input binary state (when "1" changes to "0" or vice versa) and erased portions of tape do not appear within the space of each "cell" as with the return to zero method. Thus a set of continuous ones or zeros give rise to no change of flux. This means that an accurate clocking mechanism (probably a clock track on the surface, adjacent to the data tracks) will be required, as there are no regular flux transitions on the data track to ensure that consecutive similar bits are separated out. In practice a slightly modified version of this method has been common in many applications.

NON-RETURN TO ZERO INCREMENTAL: The NRZI system encodes a "1" by a flux change and a zero by an absence of a flux change. NRZ schemes are preferable as fewer flux changes are recorded, and NRZI has the added advantage that if an error occurs, it is limited to the bit in error only, and does not also put subsequent bits wrong, as does the simple NRZ scheme. The logic for such encoding is very simple, but either an extra track of clock pulses must be recorded, or the tape must move at an extremely constant speed, for data to be recovered correctly.

PHASE ENCODING: To achieve a "self clocking" system, which can tolerate quite wide speed fluctuations (such as can occur in cassette drives) without resorting to an extra recorded track, phase encoding is employed. Simple PE recording uses a positive flux change to represent a one and a negative flux change to represent a zero. Thus both data and synchronisation information is contained in the flux change and as there will be a change for each and every bit, there will be no need for a clock. When two ones or two zeros occur in sequence an opposite flux change occurs between them and this must be masked out so that it does not appear as data. The read logic contains a timing circuit to disable the read circuit following a flux change, until after any intermediate change. (A single pulse generator would suffice,

Fig.4.2a.) Data is normally recorded in "blocks", for reasons given in the descriptions of the drive mechanisms, and the phase encoded block is preceded by a preamble of 01010101 to synchronise the data flux changes with the read circuit and its timing. The blocks are separated by gaps with no flux changes, recorded by convention in the "high" state, so that the leading zero of the preamble triggers the logic.

The BI-PHASE (MARK) system, shown as the bottom sketch of phase encoding, is a slight modification which gives a simpler logic implementation. An intermediate flux change occurs at every "cell boundary" and carries no information. This provides regular self clocking; the data is recorded by a change in mid-cell representing a "1" and the absence of a mid-cell change representing a "0". The timing circuit for bi-phase mark enables the read logic to look for a flux change (or its absence) in the mid-cell period.

Phase encoding and NRZI are the most popular systems and are the basis for the majority of internationally agreed standards. PE provides two to four times greater bit packing density than NRZI, but can reliably tolerate speed fluctuations of only 10% or so. NRZI uses simpler logic, and is used where simpler drive mechanisms are required, or where multi-track recording means that timing tracks can be tolerated. PE is preferred (even in cassette drives), as it provides the highest data density and lowest error rate, requires least bandwidth and is free from skew problems as it only needs a single track (one side of a cassette). It is commonly used with 1600 phase changes per inch (800 bpi).

7.5   MAGNETIC TAPE SYSTEMS

The magnetic tape used in computer "industry compatable" drives is made from a thin polyester, coated with an iron oxide. It is usually half an inch wide and is housed on seven to ten inch diameter spools, containing from 600 to 3600 feet of tape per spool. The main feature of a computer tape transport, which distinguishes it from an audio recorder for instance, is the near instant start, stop and reverse of tape movement. To use the tape efficiently, data is recorded in blocks, with gaps of about a half an inch in which the read/write head rests when the tape is stationary.

The read or write data transfer rate depends on the speed of tape movement and this varies with drive design and spool size. Cheap 7" spool units usually operate in the 12.5 to 25 inches per second range. Intermediate units are driven at around 45 ips. The most expensive drives use 10" spools and drive speeds from 90 to

200 ips, with 112.5 ips being a common standard. The data transfer rate also depends on the number of tracks recorded in parallel on the tape, and the recording density, which is specified in bits per inch. Although 200 bpi and 556 bpi are found in cheaper drives, 800 bpi and 1600 bpi are the industry standards. Recently super density drives have appeared, recording at 6250 bits per inch! The recording format is either NRZI or PE, and either seven (earlier standard) or nine tracks (PE) are recorded in parallel as shown in Fig.7.4. Thus a character is recorded across the tape and at 800 bpi a full tape holds more than 20 megabytes (million characters), enabling large volumes of data to be stored and to be transferred to other computers.

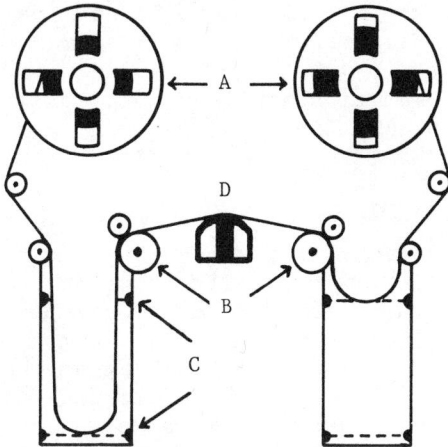

A) TAPE REEL MOTORS CONTROLLED BY (C)

B) CAPSTAN DRIVES & PINCH ROLLERS CONTROLLED BY READ-WRITE COMMAND

C) VACUUM COLUMN BUFFERS PHOTO-ELECTRIC FULL AND EMPTY SENSORS

D) READ-WRITE HEADS

FIG. 7.5 VACUUM BUFFER MAGNETIC TAPE DRIVE

An obvious problem exists with this type of drive, inertia! A full reel of tape, revolving at many thousands of revolutions per minute to achieve fast tape speed would obviously have a large inertia and would be impossible to stop or start quickly without breaking the tape. To overcome this problem a tension control system is installed, which effectively separates the tape being moved past the read/write heads (using a capstan drive and pinch roller) from the reels of tape which are driven by motors on their hubs. In slow speed drives this "buffer" of loops of tape is held by sprung mechanical tension arms. Above 45 ips these arms can not move quickly enough to avoid tape damage and then the vacuum column system shown in Fig.7.5 is used.

The reels are driven by motors which are individually controlled by photo-electric sensors indicating when the appropriate vacuum column is full or empty. Hence only a short length of tape is actually moved by the capstan drive (past the head) in response to commands from the computer to read or write. As tape is unwound from the first spool it is pulled down into the column by the vacuum. Read and write demands then cause the capstan drive to move tape from one column to the other until the take-up column indicator shows full. The take-up reel is driven until its column indicator shows empty. The three functions, supply, demand movement and take-up, all occur asynchronously with no logical connection between their circuitry. Typical start and stop times (to reach 95% of final speed) range from 2 to 16 milliseconds (45 ips $\approx$ 8 ms.) and data transfer rates vary from twenty thousand to 1.25 million bytes per second. A high speed rewind is often found on expensive drives. The tape is pulled completely out of the vacuum columns and the capstan drive pinch roller and the read/write head are lifted clear of the tape. It is then wound directly from reel to reel at very high speed.

To access data on a tape it is first started, then moved to the beginning of the required data blocks, and then the data transfer can commence. Thus the access time to recover a given piece of data is:

$$ACCESS\ TIME = STARTUP + POSITIONING + TRANSFER$$

The positioning time can be very large, a matter of some minutes! The tape is located at the start by photo sensors and a reflective marker at each end (Fig.7.4). This determines the start position for the data and stops the tape being wound beyond the far end of the tape (EOT). The only other problem which can occur (apart from dust and dirt) is tape *SKEW*. This causes the head to miscorrelate information on parallel tracks, therefore the tape must always make the same angle to the head, making roller guides necessary. Of course, the head itself must be set up accurately.

From their early days as domestic audio recorders, *CASSETTE* recorders have grown rapidly in popularity, until now they occupy a significant place in the digital data recording market. Compact, economical and easy to use, they have proved very useful as small size, serial data stores for minicomputers.

Two main types of cassette system are common. The standard "Phillips" type cassettes hold 300 feet of 0.15" wide tape in a package 4" x 2.5" x 0.5", similar to the audio type. A drive for such a cassette is shown above. A "3M" *CARTRIDGE* holds a similar length of 0.25" wide tape in a package nearly twice the size, which contains all the necessary tape guidance and tensioning equipment within it. It can be driven by a single motor, but the complexity makes the cartridge much more expensive. Cartridges do have greater bit density (1600 bpi as opposed to 800 bpi), can have four tracks, and have higher speed and data transfer rates

(30 ips and 48K bits per second).

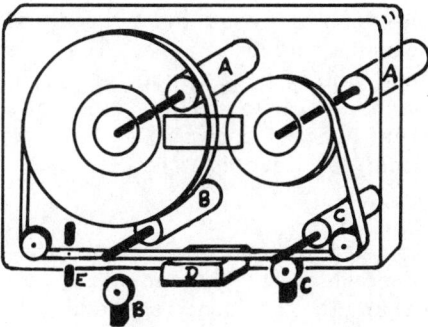

A) REEL DRIVE MOTORS

B) REVERSE DRIVE CAPSTAN
   AND PINCH ROLLER

C) FORWARD DRIVE CAPSTAN
   AND ROLLER ENGAGED

D) READ WRITE HEAD

E) ENDS OF TAPE SENSORS

FIG. 7.6 MAGNETIC CASSETTE DRIVE

The Phillips type has gained wider acceptance due to its low cost and internationally agreed standards. Both NRZI and PE encoding are possible. NRZI will tolerate speed fluctuations if a clock track is used, but this implies single side recording only and skew could be a slight problem. The international standard uses phase encoding (Fig.7.4), and blocks of data from 4 to 256 bytes long, separated by gaps and surrounded by a preamble and a postamble of 01010101. The data bytes are recorded bit serially, least significant bit first, and have two bytes of check bits added. A small pin hole in the tape provides the data end of tape marker (EOT) and it is detected by light shone through it. Transparent leader and trailer tape shows the physical ends of the tape, to stop the drive winding the tape out of the cassette.

Using this encoding process and the four motor drive shown above, two tracks can be recorded, one on each side of the tape, as with domestic cassettes. A clever system, using only the two reel drive motors and no capstans, is possible if the second track (side) is sacrificed. During tape manufacture a uniform "clock track" is recorded on the second side and this is used to control the hub drive motors to give the tape constant speed. This track only controls the speed and has nothing to do with the data which is recorded phase encoded. Cassettes can then be transferred between the two drive systems if only one side is used. The data transfer rates for cassettes are low, as the drive speeds range from 4 to 20 ips, and only about 9600 bits per second can be achieved reliably. This is adequate for many minicomputer applications.

7.6   MAGNETIC DISC DRIVES

Magnetic disc systems use the same recording principles as tape units, but a small air gap is introduced between the read/write head(s) and the disc surface. The disc is made of a light alloy, coated with a similar magnetisable layer as a tape. The disc is rotated continuously past the head and the air gap is essential to prevent wear and damage. There are two main types of disc unit, those with fixed read/write heads, and those with moving heads which often have the discs in interchangeable packs as well.

FIXED HEAD DISC: Fixed head disc units have one read/write head for each track of data to be recorded on the surface, and so usually they have fewer tracks than moving head systems. Due to closer tolerance in the manufacture of a fixed system, possibly also hermetically sealed against dust, they can have a smaller air gap and therefore a higher bit density around the track, but generally they hold less data than moving head units. The main advantage is one of speed of access to data, as the only delay is the time for one revolution of the disc, followed by the transfer time for the data. No time is wasted waiting for heads to be moved to the required track.

A magnetic drum system is conceptually the same as a fixed head disc, but has the tracks arranged on the peripheral surface of a cylindrical drum. A drum is usually faster than a disc for mechanical reasons, but small and slow drums are also made. They can attain transfer speeds in excess of 2.5 million bytes per second and can store up to 50 million bytes. An advantage over a fixed head disc is that the track length is constant, and so the bit density is constant, wheras in a disc unit the density varies with the distance from the centre. For this reason, only the outer half of a disc is ever used for data storage. A drum needs a more expensive mechanical drive and the difficulty of making a cylinder with as perfect a surface as is required is also a problem.

MOVING HEAD DISC: The attractive compromise between speed and volume of data is a moving head system and one will be found on almost every computer system above the size of the smallest minicomputers. These drives have a single head (or very occasionally a few heads) to service all the tracks on one surface. It is common to find more than one surface, so the head arrangement consists of a series of heads lined up one above the other (one per surface) as shown in Fig.7.7. Normally both sides of a disc are coated, but the heads for the undersides have been omitted for clarity. The heads are moved in and out along a radius of the disc and at a given point the rotation of the disc traces a circular *TRACK* of recorded data. If a number of surfaces are available, then the amount of data that can be accessed without any head movement is called a *CYLINDER* and consists of the current track on each surface.

The heads are moved by a moving coil linear motor. (This used to be done hydraulically.) The problem of locating the data tracks accurately enough to permit the interchangeable disc packs to be transferred to other drives has been solved by two methods. Slow speed drives, with widely spaced tracks (only one hundred to the inch or less!), use a mechanical detent mechanism, which resembles a sawn off metal comb with a ratchet to latch in one of the gaps between the teeth, to locate the heads above the tracks. This requires close tolerance manufacture to achieve compatability between drives.

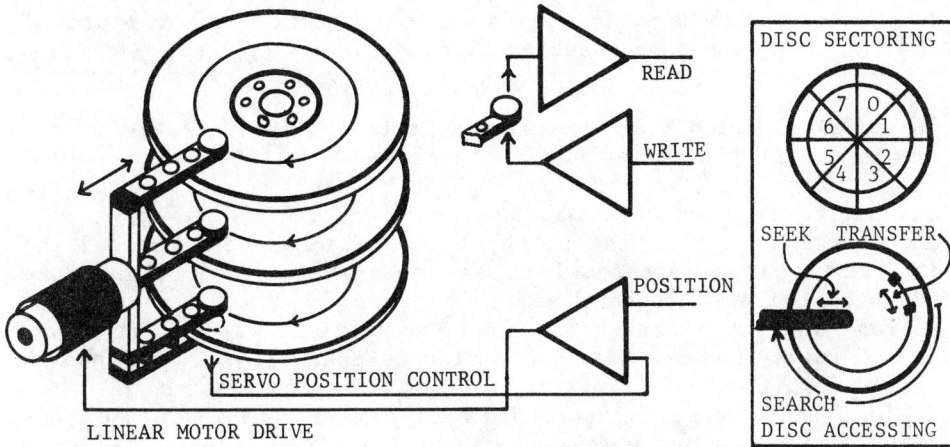

FIG. 7.7 MAGNETIC DISC DRIVE

It would be preferable to incorporate the track location information in the disc pack, so that the "compatability" was transferred with it. To do this, one surface contains a pattern to control the location of the heads on the other surfaces. It is pre-recorded (during manufacture) with alternate directions of magnetisation (in bits) on either side of the centre line of the desired data tracks for the other surfaces. (Say + just out from the track centre line, and - just inside it.) If a special narrow head is used to read this surface, a minimum signal will occur when the head is in the centre of a track and the signal will increase positively or negatively as the head moves away from the track centre line. These *SERVO* tracks are used to control the linear motor drive to make the data heads line up on the track positions. If all the read/write heads are aligned correctly,

then any disc pack can be written or read on any drive under
control from the servo surface, with the minimum of mechanical
complexity.

The heads are extremely close to the surface, the air gap being
as small as 0.1 micrometres in the highest density units. This is
about the size of the tiny particles which make "clean" smoke!
The gap is so small that the heads "fly" in the boundary layer of
air, close to the surface, and are aerodynamically designed to
maintain the gap as accurately as possible. Obviously any dust or
dirt will cause a "head crash", as the head, dust and surface
make contact, and the surface coating will be damaged, destroying
any recorded data.

The access time for data on a disc is made up of the "seek"
time for positioning the head(s) to the desired track (cylinder),
the "search" time waiting for the disc to rotate to the start of
the data, and the data transfer time.

$$ACCESS = SEEK + SEARCH + TRANSFER$$

The *LATENCY* of a disc is the average rotation (search) time, i.e.
one half of the time for a complete revolution. In normal
channel/disc arrangements the seek can be carried out without the
channel being committed, but the search requires data to be read
and checked to see if the start of the data has been reached and
the disc must be connected to the channel for this time. More
advanced drives, however, split the disc up like a cake, into
SECTORS and put a marker at each sector start, with a sensor to
detect them. Thus the search can also be done without the channel
being committed, an interrupt signalling completion of this
action, or a seek complete. This is called rotational position
sensing. Sectors are also used in simple drives (without RPS) as
a method of splitting a track up into a number of smaller, more
manageable, data records. Then they may either be fixed points on
the disc, as in Fig.7.7, or programmed start of record markers,
written as specific detectable patterns similar to tape block
preambles, giving "soft" or variable sectoring.

To gain an idea of modern disc speeds and capacities, two
examples will be quoted. The first is a simple single disc
cartridge which contains 2.5 million characters, plus format
bits, and uses mechanical track location. Data is recorded at
1100 bits/inch round the inner track and there are 100 tracks to
the inch radially, with 406 tracks in all (203 cylinders). The
disc is rotated at 1500 rpm, giving a rotation time of 40
milliseconds and a latency of 20 ms. The heads can be moved
"track to track" in 15 ms. (including settling time) and a full
radial movement takes 135 ms. with average seek time being 70ms.
This type of drive is common in minicomputer systems and can

achieve a maximum data transfer rate of 100 thousand characters per second. The second example is a high speed, high density unit found in medium-sized industrial or commercial computers. A bit density of 4000-6000 bits per inch with 200-400 tracks per inch radially provides storage of 200 million characters on each formatted pack. 20 surfaces are used, 19 for user data storage and one for servo track location patterns. Up to a thousand cylinders are accessed by average head movements taking 25 ms. (10 ms. minimum). The latency is 8.3 ms. rotational position sensing is included and the data transfer rate exceeds a million characters per second.

A very cheap disc drive, known as a floppy disc, is now widely used in minicomputer systems. Instead of a firm alloy, a flexible plastic backing is used for the disc; it has a magnetic coating on one side only and a very cheap envelope-like cover. The heads are in contact with the coating when reading or writing and are retracted if data is not read or written for 3 revolutions, to save wear. The floppy disc can be sent through the letter post, like a magnetic tape cassette. Typical floppy disc drives rotate at only 100 rpm take 10 ms. to move the head one track, and take a third of a second to move across from outer to inner tracks. With about 70 tracks and bit densities from 1000-3000 bits per inch (quite high as there is no air gap), data can be transferred at up to 9.6 thousand characters per second. The total storage available per floppy is only 1/2 million characters, but the advantage of random access to tracks at only twice the cost of cassettes (with serial access) makes the floppy disc very popular.

7.7   INTERRUPT SYSTEMS

The simplest of interrupt systems has already been mentioned in Chapter 5. This "skip-chain" method sets a single interrupt flag for any condition of a device or other hardware which must be indicated to the central control unit. It only requires microcode to detect the interrupt (before each fetch sequence), to store the program counter and machine status and to force a branch to a fixed location.

ADDRESS	MICROCODE	COMMENTS
0	$F_o.U_i.SKO$	Do not skip if interrupt set
1	RES +4	To force interrupt
2	$C_o.S_i.B_i$	No interrupt, normal fetch
3	$B_u.U_o.C_i.INC.READ$	
4	$B_o.I_i$	Fetch complete (Decode)
5	$E_i.S_i$	Disable intrp, store addr = 0
6	$C_o.B_i$	Save old program count in 0
7	$WRITE.Const[1].C_i$	Set program counter to 1
8	RES -6	Fetch start of interrupt software

FIG. 7.8 FETCH WITH INTERRUPT DETECTION

Following the transfer of control to the "interrupt handler" software, the cause of the interrupt is determined by looking at the flags in each device in turn until one is found "set".

ADDRESS	STORE CONTENT		COMMENTS
0	xx		Fixed location for storing "C"
1	XIO	SKP, Powerfail	Skip if not powerfail flag set
2	BRA	POWER	Power fail service program
3	XIO	SKP, Disc	Skip if disc flag not set
4	BRA	DISC	Disc device service routines
⋮	⋮		
21	XIO	SKP, Keyboard	Skip if keys not pressed
22	BRA	KEYIN	Keyboard service routine
23	XIO	SKP, Printer	Skip if printer flag not set
24	BRA	PRINT	Printer service routines
25	BRA	ILLEGAL	Cause of interrupt unknown

FIG. 7.9 SKIP CHAIN SOFTWARE

Following the device routine's actions to cope with the interrupt, the previous program counter "C" and the machine status are restored. The basic actions for all more complex interrupt handling mechanisms will be similar.

I1. An event occurs which causes an interrupt, setting a flag in a device, or the machine status word.
I2. Before the next instruction is fetched (if interrupts are enabled), test to see if any interrupts are pending.
I3. Disable any further interrupts, for this and any lower priority levels.
I4. Store the program counter and the machine status word if there is one.
I5. Save any active registers (and link) which may be used by a service routine.
I6. Determine the cause of the interrupt and enter the correct service routine.

After the interrupt has been processed and the required instructions executed from the service routine, steps must be taken to restore the previous program state which existed prior to the interrupt being detected.

R1. Restore any active registers (and link) which were saved at I5.
R2. Restore the program counter and other machine status saved at I4.
R3. Re-enable the interrupts for this priority level and any others which were disabled by I3.

The simple "single level non-priority" interrupt scheme would not be adequate for a computer with many interrupting devices, particularly if it is involved in time critical operations. The overhead in time, perhaps thirty instruction cycles for the skip-chain, would not be tolerable and methods must be sought to speed up the actions listed above.

The microcode used to detect the occurrence of an interrupt is as fast as can be expected; though there are methods to speed up detection the gain from them is small for a significant increase in hardware. Disabling interrupts (I3) can be done automatically by the interrupt detection microcode or in hardware which takes no extra time. Storing the machine state, program counter and active registers is one area which provides scope for improvement, some of it very ingenious. The registers must be saved at "hardware" speeds and not by STO instructions. If they are saved at fixed locations, as suggested in the simple skip-chain example, then an interrupt will not be able to interrupt an interrupt, without corrupting the original stored counter. The first solution would be to use a register "stack" with a push-down store method as described in Chapter 1. This is a satisfactory solution because an interrupt causes the active registers to be put in at the top of the stack, pushing down all those previously stored. On completion of service the registers are restored and the stack is pulled up to have the next set ready. This is not the fastest solution, nor in many ways the neatest.

If a separate set of registers were available for every interrupt (or interrupt priority level), then a simple switch from one set to another would be sufficient to save or restore a complete previous state of the central processor. This would be expensive and a more practical version of this solution is possible as a side effect of a machine implementation described in Chapter 10. All the active registers, except the program counter, are treated as store locations (called a "workspace") and are pointed to by a "workspace base register". On interrupt a switch of workspaces is made by saving the program counter (in a reserved word of the current workspace) and loading the new workspace pointer and program counter from the new set of "registers".

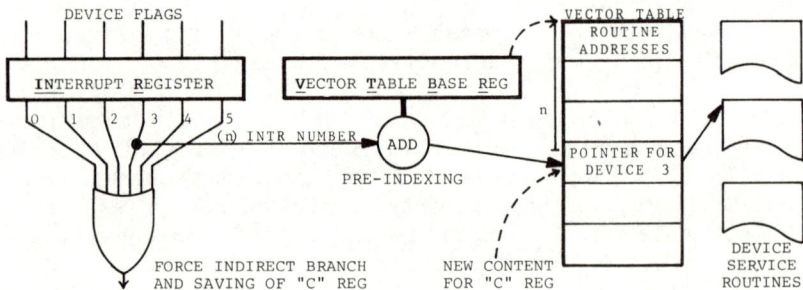

FIG. 7.10 *AUTOMATIC PRIORITY INTERRUPT*

To speed up the determination of the cause of an interrupt and entry to the correct device service program, "automatic priority" schemes are used, a simple example being shown in Fig.7.10. Such schemes move the overheads of these actions into the hardware. Instead of a special single location to which all interrupts force a branch, a separate location is used to hold the address of the service software for each different interrupt. Each device flag is connected individually to a bit of an "interrupt register" (INTR). The address of each device routine is stored in a table in the position corresponding to the number of the bit in the interrupt register to which its device is connected. On interrupt, which is caused by the OR of all the flags and is detected as before, the interrupt register is scanned and the first bit found to be set fixes the device to be serviced. Thus the order of connection of devices to the interrupt register determines the priority. The store location containing the device handler address is computed by adding the number of the bit which was found to be set to the base address of the *VECTOR TABLE*. This base address is held in a register called the "vector table base address" register (VTBR). An indirect branch forced through the calculated location transfers control to the handler.

To improve flexibility, whilst retaining a balance between speed of response to large numbers of devices and cost, a slightly modified version of the API system is commonly used. Interrupt causing devices are grouped into priorities to provide a multi-level automatic priority system. Interrupts on the same or lower priority levels are prevented from disturbing the current active level, whilst those with higher priority may interrupt. To facilitate the alteration of priorities or the deferring of an interrupt in a multi-level system each level has the bits of its interrupt register AND'ed with the corresponding bits of a mask register (MASK) before they are OR'ed together to signal an interrupt. The mask can be set by program and devices can be connected on more than one level to permit dynamic priority alteration. A simplified sketch of this system is shown in Fig.7.11. An interrupt occurring on a level higher than the one active, which also has its mask bit set, will be detected in the microcode. The device service routine is entered by a double indirection via two tables which provide complete flexibility.

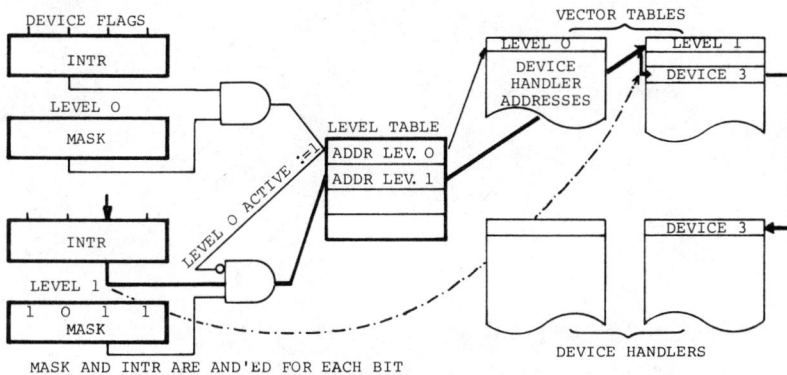

FIG. 7.11 *MULTIPLE PRIORITY LEVEL INTERRUPT*

Interrupts occur either as a result of "external" action, a device or channel completing an action or detecting an error, or because of conditions detected internally in the machine. Commonly found "internal" interrupts are: power fail, restart, parity error on store transfer (Chapter 10), protected store violation (Chapter 9) and illegal instruction. If many bits are used for the OP-code, certain combinations of bits may not have been assigned, or parts of optional hardware may not be installed, causing execution of an instruction to fail. Conditions such as overflow are sometimes indicated by an interrupt instead of just a flag.

The priority of interrupts and levels can be fixed fairly easily. Power failure and other internal failure conditions will terminate all processing and so have the highest level. The real time clock controls timing for external sampling, control outputs and system time slicing. It ranks just below failure conditions in importance. High speed peripherals such as discs interrupt frequently and require fast service if data is not to be missed; these are grouped on the next level. Low speed terminals can wait and only just out-rank the basic processing mode (running programs), which can always wait. Multiple interrupt handlers are unnecessary when using vectored priority systems, as an interrupt may interrupt an interrupt. In a similar fashion multiple copies of a device handler, for many similar terminals for instance, can be dispensed with if "sharable" code is used. Such code must be re-entrant and each new device only needs its own data area and access to the shared handler. To recap, the cause of an interrupt is determined by the skip-chain, vectored, or multi-level priority methods, and the previous machine state is saved and restored by the fixed locations, stack, or switched work areas methods.

8 Storage Media

8.1 STORAGE ELEMENTS

It has been assumed that a store can be constructed and that access to it via two registers, the store buffer register and the store address register, can be arranged using a function select of "read" or "write". To justify this assumption, the media and mechanisms will be described, starting with the necessary requirements for a basic element to be usable in a main random access store (RAS).

> 1. STORE
> It must be capable of existing in two states indefinitely.
>
> 2. WRITE
> The transitions between these states must be easily controllable.
>
> 3. READ
> The condition of the element must be easily determined.
>
> 4. RELIABILITY
> The element must be reliable, $>10^{15}$ operations, or 10^5 hours mean time between failure.
>
> 5. SIZE/POWER
> The element must be small, and consume minimal power.
>
> 6. SPEED
> Changes of state and determination of state must be fast, <1 microsecond.

The first possibility is to use ordinary registers for main store. They satisfy all criteria except 1 (if the power is turned off) and 5 (part 2). A simplified view of a single bit of a "register" store is shown in Fig.9.1. As can be seen, the only major drawback is that the store is not capable of existing in two states indefinitely, but only whilst power is connected. Such a store is said to be *VOLATILE*, whereas a store which is capable of existing indefinitely is *PERMANENT*. This problem can be partially solved in some environments by using a battery to hold the store on. This would not be suitable in more critical systems where the contents of store must never be lost.

8.2 INTEGRATED CIRCUIT STORES

These are based on the register store principle, but use modern
technology to achieve very small size and high reliability, with
very low power consumption. They are arranged in an exactly
similar fashion to "register" stores, but have different
elements. They still have the drawback of volatility. Two types
of technology are available, bipolar and MOS (metallised oxide
silicon). Bipolar transistors are similar to those used in
domestic equipment and give extremely fast, but high power
consuming circuits. MOS transistors, on the other hand, take far
less current, as they have a much higher resistance, but are
slower in operation. These conflicting requirements always hold
true, as there is a "speed power product"; to get circuits to
operate faster, more power is required.

A further division occurs between *STATIC* and *DYNAMIC* stores.
The static type, using the "cross coupled gate" principle, and
the dynamic type, retaining the state as a charged or uncharged
capacitor. The latter type requires regular refreshing to top up
the charge, as otherwise it will leak away over a period of time.
Fig.8.1a shows a static element made of MOS transistors. The two
resistors at the top are actually constructed as transistors,
connected as in Fig.8.1b, to simplify construction, because they
are easier to make and smaller than the equivalent resistors.

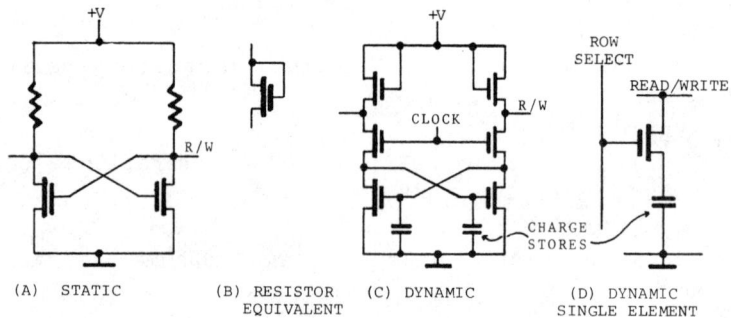

(A) STATIC   (B) RESISTOR   (C) DYNAMIC   (D) DYNAMIC
                    EQUIVALENT   SINGLE ELEMENT

FIG. 8.1 *INTEGRATED CIRCUIT STORE ELEMENTS*

Operation is the same as the "RS" bistable and conceptually the
same arrangement as the "register" store is used. The
disadvantage of the static store is that it consumes power all
the time; to minimise power consumption, the change to Fig.8.1c,
a dynamic store, is made. The operation of the upper two
transistors has changed, so that they now disconnect power from
the bistable except when clocked. The bistable (lower two
transistors) operates using the charge in the capacitors to hold
it in the set or reset state. One capacitor is charged up and the
other discharged storing the "1" or "0" state. The disadvantage

of the dynamic store is that the charge "leaks" out of the capacitors, so every few milliseconds the clock has to be pulsed for each element (every address in store), to connect the power supply and top up the capacitor.

The simplest possible store element of the dynamic type is shown in Fig.8.1d, and it contains just a capacitor, charged or discharged, and a single transistor to isolate it from the outside world except when reading, writing or refreshing. The simplicity of the element means that more of them may be packed into one integrated circuit, but more complex accessing and refreshing circuitry is required. Access times vary from a few nanoseconds for the fastest static bipolar store to 500 nanoseconds for the slowest MOS dynamic store, which also requires refresh pulses every few milliseconds. No access is possible during the refresh cycle. Integrated circuits containing IK bits of static RAS and 4K bits of dynamic RAS are now common and 16K bit dynamic circuits are under laboratory evaluation.

8.3   MAGNETIC CORE STORAGE

The third possibility, and until recently the most common computer store, uses small "cores" of a magnetic substance, usually ferrite, with wires threading the annuli. The cores are very small (less than 1mm outside diameter) and the two states are the different directions of magnetisation, clockwise, or anti-clockwise around the annulus. Two main factors control the speed of switching of a "core", the current drive (force to switch) and the size. Thus, assuming the same material and some sensible limit on the current, the smaller the core, the faster it will be.

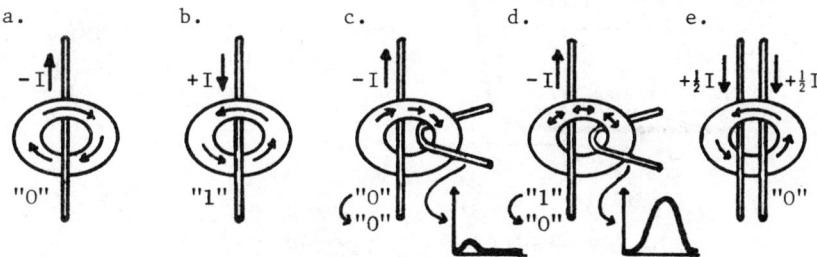

FIG. 8.2 OPERATION OF CORE ELEMENTS

The transitions between states are easily controlled. By applying the opposite polarity current through a wire threaded through the core, the direction of magnetisation is reversed, and the core is left in the other state. This is shown in Fig.8.2a and b. When no current is applied, the core remains in its current state and therefore is a permanent store. The transition between states for a ferrite material is shown on the *HYSTERESIS* curve (often called a B-H loop) in Fig.8.3. It is nearly "square" for ferrites giving well defined states. The magnetising force (H) is proportional to the algebraic sum of the currents passing in any wires through a core, as in Fig.8.2e, and the magnetisation (B) or "flux" in the core is plotted against this.

Detecting the state of a core is the first drawback of the system. The state of a core can only be detected easily by changing its state and detecting the resulting current in a *SENSE* winding. The current on a wire causes a change in the magnetisation of the core and this "flux change" induces current to flow in a sense winding. Thus, current would flow if the change were from "1" to "0", but not if the core was a "0" already. A reverse current is also induced on the wire which is being used to change the state of the core. This means that a greater drive current will be necessary to overcome this reverse current; this effect is used to advantage in a more complex core store described further on. In practice, as the hysteresis loop is not "square", current does flow if the core was in the "0" state previously. Fig.8.2c and d shows that the time and voltage difference between the small "0" pulse and large "1" pulse, though both are only millivolts, is adequate to determine which cores were in which state.

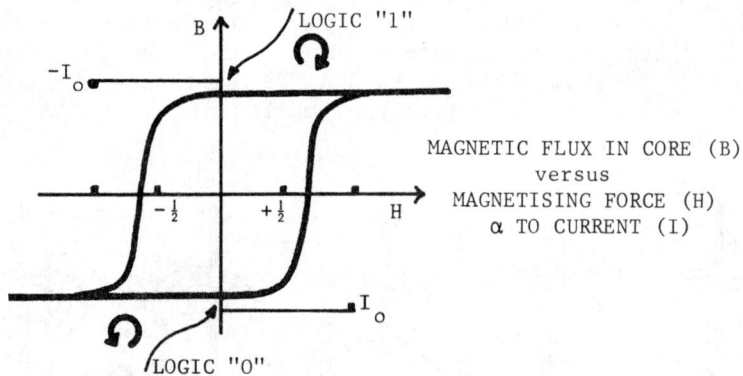

FIG 8.3 *FERRITE CORE HYSTERESIS CURVE*

Reading the state of a core is achieved at the expense of destroying the information stored in it. This information must be held in the store buffer register temporarily, whilst it is written back to restore the core to its original state. This is termed *DESTRUCTIVE* readout, and the storage cycle is always a read/write cycle, as reading involves a write back, and writing is preceded by a read, discarding the contents, to set all cores in a word to zero prior to setting the new states. Note the difference between the read/write cycle, the read or write micro commands, and read or write XIO functions.

To limit the pulses produced by cores which were in the "0" state prior to reading (caused by the non-square B-H curve) and from those cores which were unselected, yet received one half of the switching current, the cores in a plane are tilted in alternate directions and the sense wires are threaded so that the polarity of half of the small "noise" pulses is opposite to that of the other half, tending to cancel each other. Use must be made of the time difference between generation of the "1" pulse and all other pulses, to ensure correct reading. A strobe pulse, of very short duration samples the voltage on the sense wire when the "1" pulse would be expected and its presence or absence fixes the read state of the core.

Typical figures for a core store are: cycle time 500ns, read time 200ns, total drive current 400mA, output pulse on reading 20mV. Core diameter 1/2mm. Core storage is reliable and amply proven over many years and meets the requirement for reliability. Cores are small and consume NO power when storing, only a small amount being necessary when a core is switched to read or write the contents. Core stores are made with cycle times of 500 nanoseconds to 2 microseconds, the slower stores using larger, cheaper cores, with the wiring through them being simpler. MOS integrated circuit stores and core stores are both popular as computer stores, as each has particular advantages. Between them they dominate the market.

8.4 READ ONLY STORAGE

A slightly different set of criteria applies for ROS, in that though it must be permanent, it does not need controllable transitions between states and only reading need be fast. It must be possible to "program the store" in the first place; this can either be done during manufacture, when the contents to be held will be "wired" in (mask programmable), or in the field by providing the ability to fix "0" or "1" states (programmable read only store, PROS). One method which is used is the fusable link (Nichrome). All elements can be taken to "0" or "1" levels by "fuses" and the required ones are "blown" by application of a suitable voltage, to give the store its content as shown in Fig.8.4. This method is sometimes altered, so that the fuses are not blown but changed from a non-conducting state to a conducting state by altering their crystalline structure. The process can be reversed by application of ultra-violet light, thus giving an erasable programmable read only store or EPROS.

A method, using magnetic coupling as the store, is also shown in Fig.8.4. It is very robust and can be used in adverse environments. In operation, a pulse is driven down the selected address line and the desired word is produced on the sense lines, ones and zeros depending on whether the wire passes through the core or not. It is similar to the 2D word organised core store described in the next chapter, except that the cores are very much larger to accommodate all the wires.

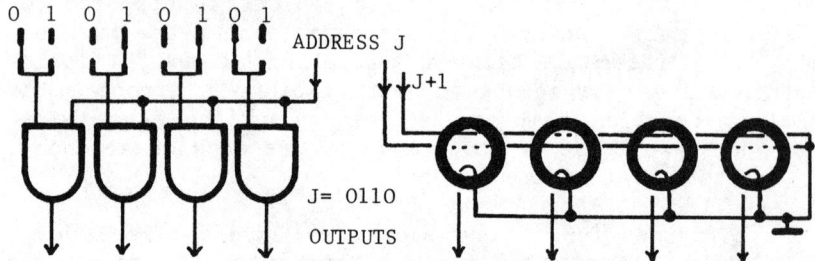

FIG. 8.4 *READ ONLY STORE ELEMENTS*

Another type of ROS is a simple optical store where the bit patterns forming the words are stored as holes in an opaque film. A laser is used to burn the holes to program the store. A photo-detector is used to read the store, indicating "0" or "1" by detecting light shone onto the film, passing through the holes. ROS are available in so many different media that no definitive figures can be given, but optical stores read in a few nanoseconds, semiconductor stores in a few tens of nanoseconds, and magnetic stores in a hundred nanoseconds or more.

9 Storage Arrangements

9.1 INTEGRATED CIRCUIT STORES

It is reasonably simple to provide a "random access" store (RAS) using the integrated circuit elements described in Chapter 8. If one of the "static" elements is used it will be an even simpler task, because no circuits will be required for periodic refreshing of the stored charges.

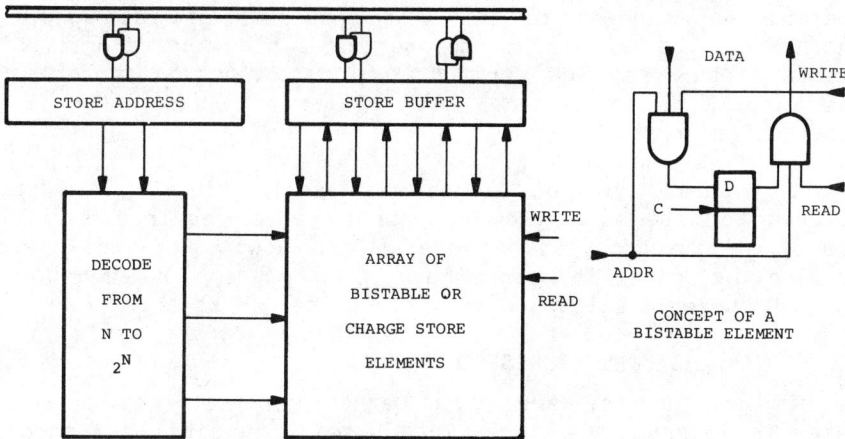

FIG. 9.1 *INTEGRATED CIRCUIT STORE ARRANGEMENT*

A number of bistable elements are normally grouped together to form a "word" which is then treated as a single entity throughout the storage system. The grouping of eight bits to give "byte-addressable" storage is also common. Stores which treat each bit seperately to give "bit-addressability" can provide significant advantages, but at the expense of much extra decoding and addressing logic. Such advantages can be obtained more easily by using a word organised store and then microcoding to subdivide the word into bits. Each addressable unit, be it word, byte or bit, needs a unique "address" with which it can be referenced. This address is held in the store address register "S" described in Chapter 4. It must be decoded into an individual select line, which connects to all the bits forming the word, to enable them to be selected from all the other groups of bits in the store. If a store is to contain 4096 words, each containing 16 bits, then a decoder from a twelve bit address to 4096 individual select lines is required. This is similar to the simple three bit to eight line decoder of Fig.4.1, but on a much larger scale. Fabricated using integrated circuit techniques, its repetitive structure makes it less difficult to produce than might appear at first.

The "read" lines from each element are connected, as are the "write" lines. The data inputs and outputs for each element are connected to the output and input of the corresponding bit of the store buffer register "B". The action of the store shown in Fig.9.1 is then quite simple.

The address of the desired word is put to the store address register and acts as input to the decoder logic which sets the correct line "true". This enables all the logic associated with the desired word, but leaves all other words disabled. The "read" line can be selected to enable the outputs of the word, the content of the location, to be set into the store buffer register. Otherwise the "write" line is selected to force the elements of the word to the same states as the content of the store buffer register.

If a dynamic type of element is used, then logic must be included to cope with the "refresh" cycles required every few tens of milliseconds. With the examples shown in Fig.8.1c and d the clock or row select lines have to be pulsed for each word to "top-up" those capacitors which are in the "1" state.

9.2   2D AND 3D CORE STORES

The simplest way of arranging magnetic cores into a storage system is to group the cores into words in a similar fashion to the "word-organised" IC store. Two wires - a *DRIVE* wire and a *SENSE* wire - then thread through each core. Each drive wire threads all the cores in the same word and each sense wire threads all the cores which represent the same bit in each word. Thus for a store of 4096 words, each of 16 bits, there will be 4096 drive wires and 16 sense wires.

To read a word from this store the mechanism described in Chapter 8 is employed. The address of the word is put into the store address register and is decoded to select the correct word. The true logic signal from the decoder is fed to a "word drive amplifier" which amplifies it to produce a pulse sufficient to change any core in the "1" state to the "0" state. This pulse is driven along the word drive line by the amplifier. A suitably timed "strobe" input enables the sense amplifiers connected to the sense lines. The small detected pulses are converted into zero and one logic states by the sense amplifier and this pattern (the value of the addressed word) is stored in the store buffer register "B" as is shown in Fig.9.2. The word is available for reading by the rest of the computer but as a destructive readout process has been employed, the word has all been set to the zero state, and will have to be restored by a write operation.

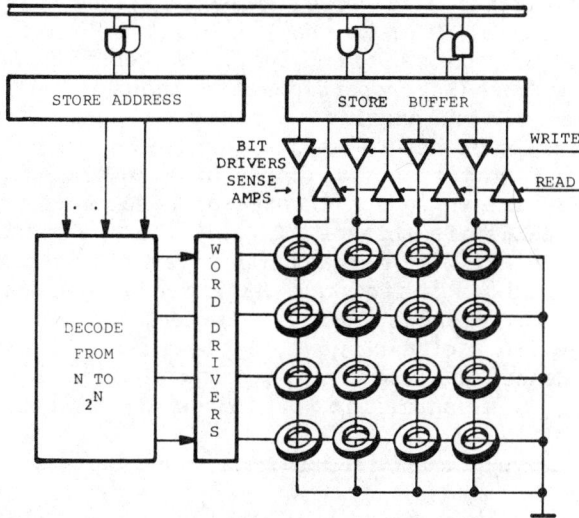

FIG. 9.2 CORE STORE, 2D ARRANGEMENT

To write into an all zero word the word drive line is again selected by the address decoder, but the pulse from the drive amplifier is of the opposite polarity to that used for reading and is one half of the magnitude necessary to switch a core from the zero to the one state. The sense amplifiers are not needed during a write operation, but the sense line is used to function as a bit drive line. The data in the store buffer register is fed to bit drive amplifiers which produce no pulse if a bit is to be left in the "0" state, or a further one half switching pulse if a bit is to be set to the "1" state. This uses coincident currents (described in Chapter 8) to give a large enough pulse to switch the chosen pattern of bits to the "1" state. The write operation, or restore after destructive read, is complete and a further store operation may be started. In practice a write operation commences with a destructive read to erase any previous content of the word prior to writing in the new bit pattern.

The two-dimensional (2D) core store system is so called because it is a single plane of cores, "N" words of "M" bits. The advantage of this simple system is that only two wires thread each core. The cores can be small and hence will switch more quickly. It is possible to make the plane and thread the wires mechanically as there are only two. The disadvantage is that all the decoding is done by logic outside the plane. This also implies that a seperate drive amplifier is needed for each word which would make it appear an expensive system.

The "three-dimensional" core storage system has four wires threading each core. It uses the principle of coincident current selection, relying on the fact that the force trying to change the state of a core is proportional to the algebraic sum of the currents in all wires passing through the core. The four wires shown in Fig.9.3 each have a unique purpose:
1. The X wire threads all cores of a row in every plane
2. The Y wire threads all cores of a column in every plane
3. The SENSE wire threads all cores in one plane
4. The INHIBIT wire threads all cores in one plane

The system is bit organised and "3D" because it consists of a plane of cores to store the first bit of each word, a plane to store the second bit of each word, a plane for all the third bits and so on. Hence for the example used before there would be sixteen planes each containing 4096 cores arranged as a square of 64 cores by 64.

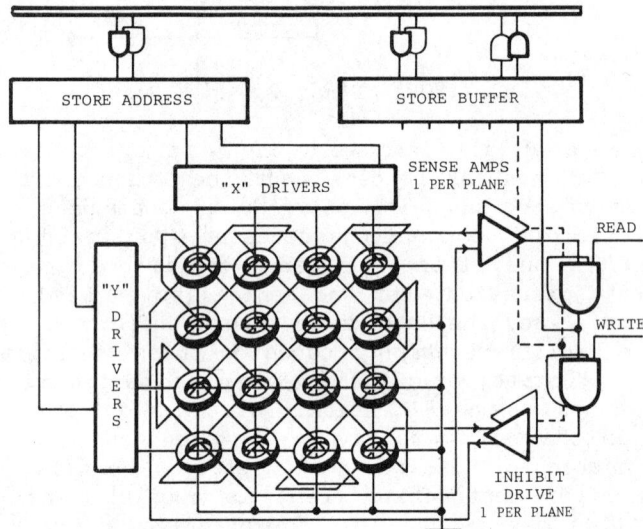

FIG. 9.3 CORE STORE, 3D ARRANGEMENT

To read from the store, the address of the required word is put into the store address register and is treated as two half addresses. Each is fed via a decoder to the "X" and "Y" drivers respectively. The decoders are much smaller than in a "2D" system as they decode from "N/2" as opposed to "N" for an address of N bits. Also fewer drivers are required (128 not 4096). One core (and only one) from each plane will be selected by both an X drive and a Y drive and these cores form the word. The X and Y drivers supply a pulse of one half of that necessary to switch a core from the one state to the zero state. A chosen word of cores will be selected by coincident current and will switch, producing small pulses on the sense wires. The strobed sense amplifier for each plane detects either a tiny "zero-state" pulse or a small "one-state" pulse as the cores switch, and sets the corresponding bit in the store buffer register accordingly. All cores in the planes which did not receive coincident X and Y drives either receive no drive and so generate no pulse, or receive only one drive and produce a small "disturb" pulse which is similar to a zero-state and is ignored by the strobing of the sense amplifier.

The destructive readout problem is encountered again and a write-back is necessary. The X and Y drivers selected by the address remain the same, as does the magnitude of the drive pulse. Only its polarity changes from negative to positive. Thus all the bits in the word would be switched to the "1" state. The "inhibit" drivers are used to override this to obtain the correct bit pattern. If a "1" state is desired then the inhibit driver is not enabled and no current is driven along the inhibit wire. This leaves the coincident "X-Y" drive to write a "1". If a zero is required then a half current of opposite polarity to the X and Y drives is driven down the inhibit wire. This reduces the total switching current in the core so that it is insufficient to write a "1", thus it is left as a zero.

The wires in a 3D system have unique uses and so the drive amplifiers are less complex to design and construct. The sense lines could also be used as a check during a write operation in the same way as for reading if a register was provided to hold the checking outputs. As much of the selection is done by coincident currents on the planes, many fewer drive amplifiers are needed and the system would appear to be cheaper. The disadvantages are that the cores have to be larger (hence slower) and mechanical threading is not possible. The pattern of wires shown in Fig.9.3 is desirable in order to minimise the "disturb" pulses and for other reasons, and the two extra wires are the ones which are hand threaded.

A number of compromises which retain the advantages of "on-plane" selection yet use only three (or even only two) wires through each core are possible. As they are compromises between two-dimensional and three-dimensional systems they are termed "two and a half" dimensional (2.5D). If checking on write can be forgone then during a write half cycle the sense wire is unused. The inhibit wire could be omitted and the sense wire made to double up as sense for reading and inhibit for writing. This would require only three wires per core, but at the expense of more sophisticated, combined sense-amplifier/inhibit-drivers.

<u>2D</u>   WORD organised

READ   word drive -I   detect on sense line
WRITE word drive I/2   bit drive 0 or I/2
Many drive amplifiers; large, external decoder;
small core size, mechanical threading (2 wires).

<u>3D</u>   BIT organised

READ   X drive -I/2, Y drive -I/2, detect on sense
WRITE X drive +I/2, Y drive +I/2, inhbt -I/2 or 0
Few drive amplifiers; small external decoders;
large core size; hand threading; 4 wires per core.

<u>2.5D</u> BIT organised

READ   X drive -I/2, Y drive -I/2, detect on sense
                 line or by impedance difference
WRITE X drive +I/2, Y drive 0 or +I/2
            (or inhibit on sense wire if 3 wires)
Compromise; few but complex drives/sense/inhibit;
small core; mechanical threading; 2 or 3 wires.

FIG. 9.4 COMPARISON OF CORE SYSTEMS

A further reduction to two wires per core, retaining the bit organisation, needs two complex circuits. These must allow sensing and inhibiting to be carried out on the X or Y wires as well as their primary addressing function. Cores switching from the "1" state show a higher impedance to the drive wires than those which were switching from the "0" state. This is because more energy is used up, as is shown in the hysteresis curve in Fig.8.3. A core in the "1" state produces a larger pulse on the sense wire, but this pulse must also be induced on every other wire running through the core, even the drive wires. The pulse is of the opposite polarity to the drive (a back EMF) and so the core appears to have a higher impedance than one which was in the "0" state initially. One can dispense with the sense wire by designing a clever driver which can also detect whether it is driving a slightly higher impedance. (Impedance is equivalent to resistance but for A.C. or pulses.) The inhibit function must also be transferred to the drive wires and this is arranged by inhibiting all the drivers of one side (say Y) on a given plane if a zero state is to be written, and not inhibiting them if a one is wanted. Logic external to the plane performs this and would use modern implementational methods. The extra complexity of sensing or inhibiting whilst driving can be offset against smaller, faster cores and threading done by machine.

9.3   ARRANGEMENTS FOR SPEED

Store systems are organised to be bit, byte or word addressable and have an *ACCESS* time and a *CYCLE* time. The organisation of store systems determines the quantity of data which can be addressed by an instruction (bit, byte, or word). The number of bits (or "width") of the data bus between the store and the control unit fixes the amount of data fetched or stored during each store access, and is often, though not necessarily, fixed by the store organisation. The access time refers to the time taken to retrieve "width" bits of data from store and place them in the store buffer register ready for the control unit. The cycle time, on the other hand, refers to the period of time a store requires between the start of a read or write operation and the start of a subsequent operation on the same store location. This obviously includes the "write-back" for a core store system.

The basic speed of a store system is determined by the two factors of cycle time and bus width, and provides a data rate in millions of bits per second which may be used for comparison. The example of store arrangement which has been used has 4096 words, each of 16 bits. A typical core system might have a bus width of 16 bits and a cycle time of one microsecond (access 500 ns). A similar semiconductor store might have similar access time and bus width, but the cycle time would also be about 500 nanoseconds as no restore is necessary. If a given store mechanism has been chosen, with a given "cycle" time, and it is found that this raw speed is inadequate for the application, how can it be made to appear faster?

A worthwhile speed advantage may be gained by providing a small *SCRATCHPAD* store. This consists of some fast registers, similar to the accumulator and general purpose registers, and is used to retain frequently used data and partial results. There would be from 16 to 128 locations of scratchpad store which would be from 10 to 100 times faster than the main store. Two arrangements are possible for the method of access to a scratchpad. One is to provide special instructions which only address the scratchpad, and as there are relatively few locations it would be possible to have a "double address" format. The other arrangement is for the scratchpad to take the form of the first "N" locations of the normal addressable space and so any access using these locations would be very fast. The advantage of a scratchpad is the greater speed of store access for some regularly used locations, whilst the disadvantages are the extra cost and complexity, and the limitation in size. This is bound to cause special cases which will prevent the average programmer (writing in a high level language) using it to advantage.

A scratchpad could be arranged in the form of a "stack", as described in Chapter 1. Speed improvement could be obtained, without introducing special cases, with a "zero address" format implying the use of the top locations of the stack. However, this is not the primary reason for using a stack: it is usually employed to give a machine a more logical structure and to simplify its use, although the speed gain can be had as well. Such machines are not very common, though no good reason for this is apparent.

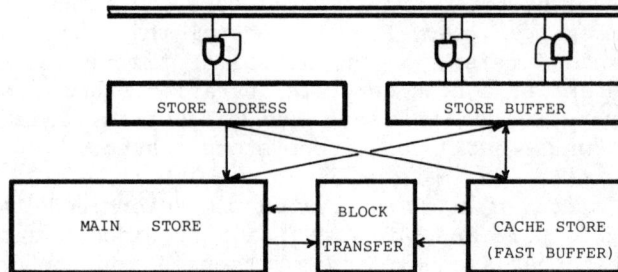

FIG. 9.5 BUFFER STORE ARRANGEMENT

On big computer systems which have large main stores it is possible to have only a relatively small part "fast", yet still have the whole system appear fast. The control unit can address both the small fast store and the bulk of slower cheaper store for which accesses will appear slow. To give the performance of a faster store the majority of accesses must be to the faster part of store. This is arranged by moving program and data so that the currently active parts reside in the fast buffer store. The term *CACHE* store is also used for such systems. Transfers are made between main and buffer stores in blocks with a large bus width to ensure a high transfer rate. When a data word or instruction is accessed which is not found in the fast store, the whole block containing the word is copied to it. This guarantees that for normal sequential type programs and normal array or matrix data, the majority of accesses are to the fast buffer. The term cache tends to be used for systems which transfer a smaller size of block than in a buffer store system. This can give a greater "hit rate" if the program and data are more random.

The buffer store can also be used to give an increase in the volume of store which can be purchased for a given outlay: a sketch of the system is shown in Fig.9.5. Typical job mix results show that from 10-20% of accesses are made to main store (in a particular job environment) with a buffer of eight thousand words and a main store of 128 thousand. If the buffer had an access time of 250 ns. and the main store one of 2 microseconds, then the apparent speed would be 400 ns. under these conditions.

For core stores and other destructive readout systems, the write back necessary after each read access is wasted time. For read only operations the next store access could start as soon as the read half cycle had finished, if the store addressing mechanism were duplicated. This occurs when an instruction is read down to the instruction register. Decoding should commence immediately and if a store cycle is required for execution, it could be started. The gain could approach a doubling in apparent speed at this point. Note that even if the store address mechanism is not duplicated, decoding and execution of an instruction should always commence at the end of the "access" rather than at the end of the "cycle". Further study of this type of overlapping led to the idea of interleaved modules of storage.

If the store is split into more than one part, then accesses can be directed to different "modules" of store, each with completely separate store access and buffer registers. This would give (roughly) a halving of access time for two or more modules. The addresses are arranged so that even addresses appear in one module and odd ones in the other. A second store access can be started in one module whilst one is in progress (even in its read part) in the other. High level language programming will not enable full advantage to be taken of this arrangement, as it will not permit the optimisation of instruction and operand placement to ensure that the next word required is always in the "other" module. The most popular of the speed enhancing methods, after the possibilities for easy overlaps have been exploited, is the buffer/cache system. It is found in most large computers.

9.4   ARRANGEMENTS FOR VOLUME

The normal method of increasing the available volume (size) of storage is to add some form of store which is significantly cheaper than main store when arranged to store large numbers of words. Any further block of storage which is not normally directly addressable by the programmer via the normal instruction set is referred to as "auxiliary" store. It may take many forms, but if it is implemented using a moving store, usually a disc or drum, it is called a *BACKING* store. Transfers can only be done between the main and backing stores in blocks, and the words in the backing store are not directly addressable by instruction. It is much slower than main store, but is much cheaper per bit and is capable of storing hundreds of megabytes. Such an extension is also possible on a reduced scale using a non-moving medium.

Extended store, normally extended core store or ECS, is a large bank of slow access storage hung onto the back of main store. The control unit is only able to access ECS to transfer large blocks of data to or from main store. The addressable range of instructions does not include ECS. The block size is fairly large for efficiency and could be 1024 words or more. Implementation from large cores in a 2.5D arrangement would be suitable from speed and cost criteria. It is convenient to arrange for all input-output to be performed to and from the ECS to avoid cycle stealing problems. If the control unit is able to address locations of the extended store directly, then a different term is used.

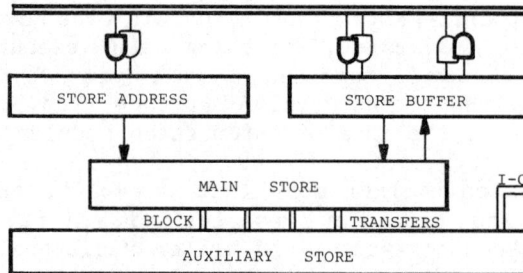

FIG. 9.6 *EXTENDED STORAGE*

Large core store, LCS, is conceptually very similar to the buffer store described before, but involves adding a large block of slow store, rather than a small block of fast store, to the medium speed main store. The control unit can directly address all the store, as well as control block transfers between the levels. A multi-level store can be implemented to include LCS, main and cache store. This permits data and instructions to be located in the store so that the access time is inversely proportional to the frequency of access. However, this desirable state of affairs (from cost vs. speed vs. store size standpoint) can be made more rational.

Software overlay systems are designed to use a two or more level storage system, particularly including backing store, to achieve a much increased usable store size for the programmer. This is obtained with fixed resources by accepting occasional losses in speed. An example will be used to describe how an overlay system works.

A programmer writes a program and discovers it is too large to fit in the main store of the machine in which it is to run. The program consists of many procedures (routines), some of which are very seldom used and some of which always follow in a set sequence. This logical program division can be used to subdivide it into sections called "overlays". A pattern of which sections will overlay which others can be arranged. A simple program could contain four parts which are executed as a sequential cycle. These could be input (A), calculation (B), output (C), and further calculation (D), after which (A) is run again. On commencing, the main store is loaded with A and B, and copies of all four parts are held on backing store. After executing A and B the operating system software would copy A out to the disc and copy C into the main store to overlay A. D would overlay B in a similar fashion and the appearance of a large store is achieved at the expense of disc space and transfers. Of course, much expertise is needed to arrange the variable sized sections to fit neatly over each other in the main store.

A similar technique is used on infrequently used routines, which may be defined by the programmer as "load on call". They would only be loaded into store, in a common shared area, if and when they are accessed. Such systems are common on small machines, but as they cause overheads to the system and demand careful use by programmers, hardware is designed to provide automatic overlays.

9.5 VIRTUAL STORAGE SYSTEMS

Virtual storage implies a store management mechanism whereby hardware automatically provides a large contiguous address space to the user, yet requires a much smaller "real" store in which to run. No prespecification is required of the overlays. Instead the program and data are considered as a "virtual space", which is split up into equal, fixed sized *PAGES*, of 4K words for instance. A copy of the complete virtual space is held in the backing store. The real main store is subdivided into *PAGE FRAMES* of the same size as the pages. During execution any page from the virtual space can reside in any page frame in the real store. The necessary mapping must be handled so that the address of the page frame is substituted for the page address, for all accesses. This "dynamic address translation" (DAT) is handled by hardware and the complete system is often referred to as "paging". Obviously there are problems when a page is accessed which is not in the real store, and a detailed example shows how they are overcome.

Each virtual address consists of two parts: the page address and the offset of a word within a page. Each real or "effective" address also has two parts: the offset of a word within a page frame, which is the same as the virtual offset, and the page frame address. The offset is unchanged by the DAT. When a store access commences, the complete virtual address is presented to the control unit. The control unit uses the virtual page address as a displacement down a table of entries, one for each page.

This is called the "page table" and is held in store and pointed to by the "page table base register" (PTBR). There is an entry in the page table for each virtual page, starting with page zero and going through to the end of the possible virtual address space. The length of this table and the size of backing store are the only practical limits to the virtual store. The entry for each page contains four fields:

1. A presence bit, indicating if the page is in store
2. The location of the page, in real or backing store
3. A write marker bit to show a changed page
4. An optional protection key: see Section 9.6

If the entry given by the page displacement added to the contents of the PTBR has its presence bit set, the page is in real store. The address portion of the table entry is substituted for the page address, giving the effective address which is put in the store address register. If the presence bit is not set, however, the operating system uses the address given to fetch in the page from backing store. A page will have to be replaced, the table entries updated, and the new effective address computed as before to let the access be completed.

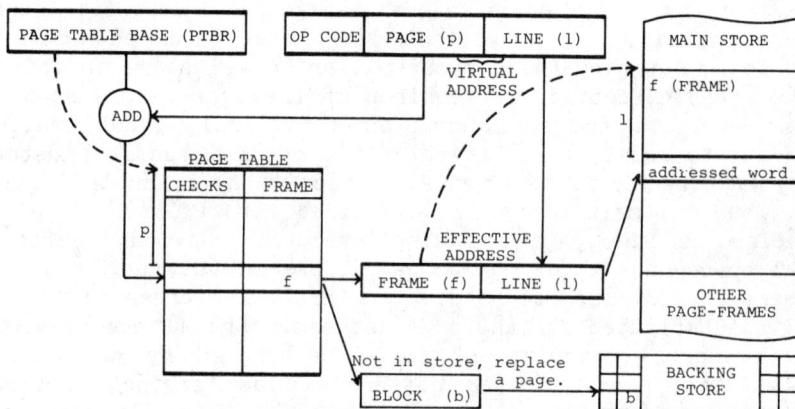

FIG. 9.7 PAGING HARDWARE FOR VIRTUAL STORAGE

Page replacement algorithms have been studied a lot: some of those used are first in first out, least recently used, and biased first in first out. All can perform well under many circumstances, and can also fail dismally. If a page is chosen for replacement its write marker is checked, and only if it has been altered is it written out to backing store to overwrite the copy held there. No knowledge of the system is required to be able to use the large virtual address space, though it obviously helps the system's performance if programs do not branch about all over the place or access data on random pages, causing lots of "page faults" and even "thrashing".

9.6   STORE PROTECTION

One type of protection is a physical check that the data is actually what was stored. This is discussed in Chapter 10. The type of store protection meant here is the type which stops programs accessing each other, or even overwriting themselves. Any store protection scheme must be implemented in hardware or it will be possible to circumvent it, either deliberately or accidently. Protection types are:

1. No access, except by authorisation code
2. Execute only, may be used as an instruction only
3. Read only, precludes execution, e.g. constant data
4. Read and execute only
5. Read and write only, precludes execution
6. Write only, but someone else must read!
7. No protection

The write only case would seem stupid, but with authorisation codes as well it can make more sense. All of the main types may have an authorisation code as well, and this is known as "key" protection. The key may hold only for one word, but this would be prohibitively expensive so it is usual to have a key for each block (or page) of store.

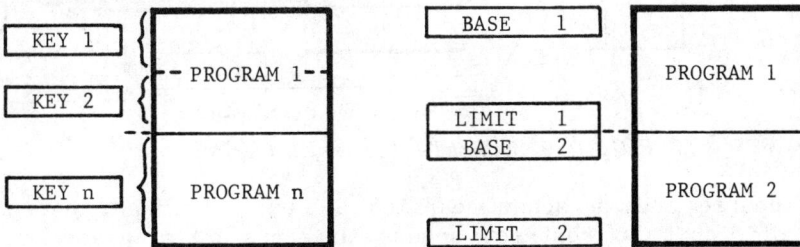

FIG. 9.8 *PROTECTION MECHANISMS*

A different type of protection is to use the address itself as its own protection. All programs start at location zero and then have a "base address" added. This total is then compared with a "limit" and only accesses within the range are permited. This is shown in Fig.9.8. Logically, programs too may be split into "segments", and it would seem sensible to allow the checking to be done for each segment separately. If a key were added as well, a very high degree of security could be assured. Fig.9.9 shows the complete store access arrangement for "segmentation with paging".

The address of a word now contains its segment, page and offset. The segment field added to the contents of the "segment table register" points to a segment table entry. Each segment has an entry in the segment table which contains four fields:

1. A presence bit for the segment's page table
2. The base address of the segment
3. The limit address of the segment
4. Protection bits and authorisation code

The protection bits and authorisation are checked and if agreement is found the page table is indexed down by the virtual page address. If the paging hardware scores a "hit", the dynamic address translation takes place and the store is accessed.

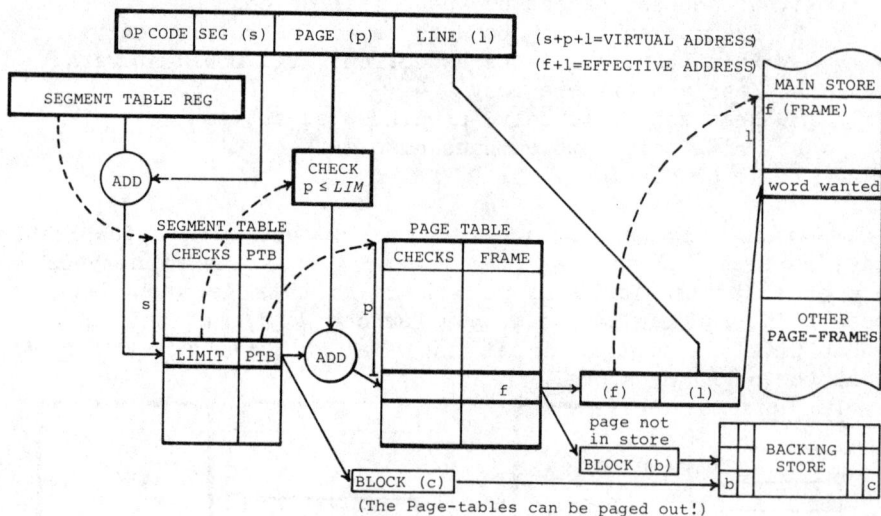

FIG. 9.9 *SEGMENTATION WITH PAGING*

Of course such a scheme carries a large overhead, but it is very difficult to restrict access to parts of programs or data without such problems.

10 Computers, Communication and Reliability

10.1 A COMPLETE COMPUTER

Returning to the original five block structure, a complete computer system may be constructed from the parts which have been discussed individually. There are still differences in the ways the blocks may be connected, and the two main methods are shown in Fig.10.1. In considering the control unit and the arithmetic and logic unit, one main bus and two subsidiary internal busses (for ALU inputs) were used. The problem of organising the machine externally for the greatest utility of the internal structure remains. The external bus mechanism can be arranged with separate input-output and store busses, or with a single bus for both functions, sometimes called a "unibus".

A two bus machine will be faster for work not involving input-output operation, but will not be so versatile. All peripheral transfers, even just from one peripheral to another, will have to go into and out of the main store. A single bus machine will be able to transfer from one device to another without using the store. It will need more complex controllers for the peripherals and will tend to be slower for normal store use. The single bus system does, however, allow all input output to be done from store locations directly, thus removing the requirement for special instructions for this. A device controller looks directly at the store locations it is allocated, to check if any action is required. Transfers then proceed between the device and the store locations designated for its data.

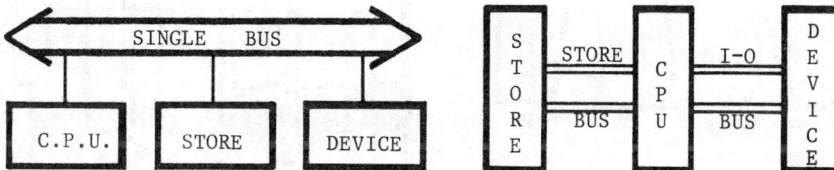

FIG. 10.1 BUS STRUCTURES

Machine detail also differs in other ways. The control unit can be modified to have two modes. The instruction set is then

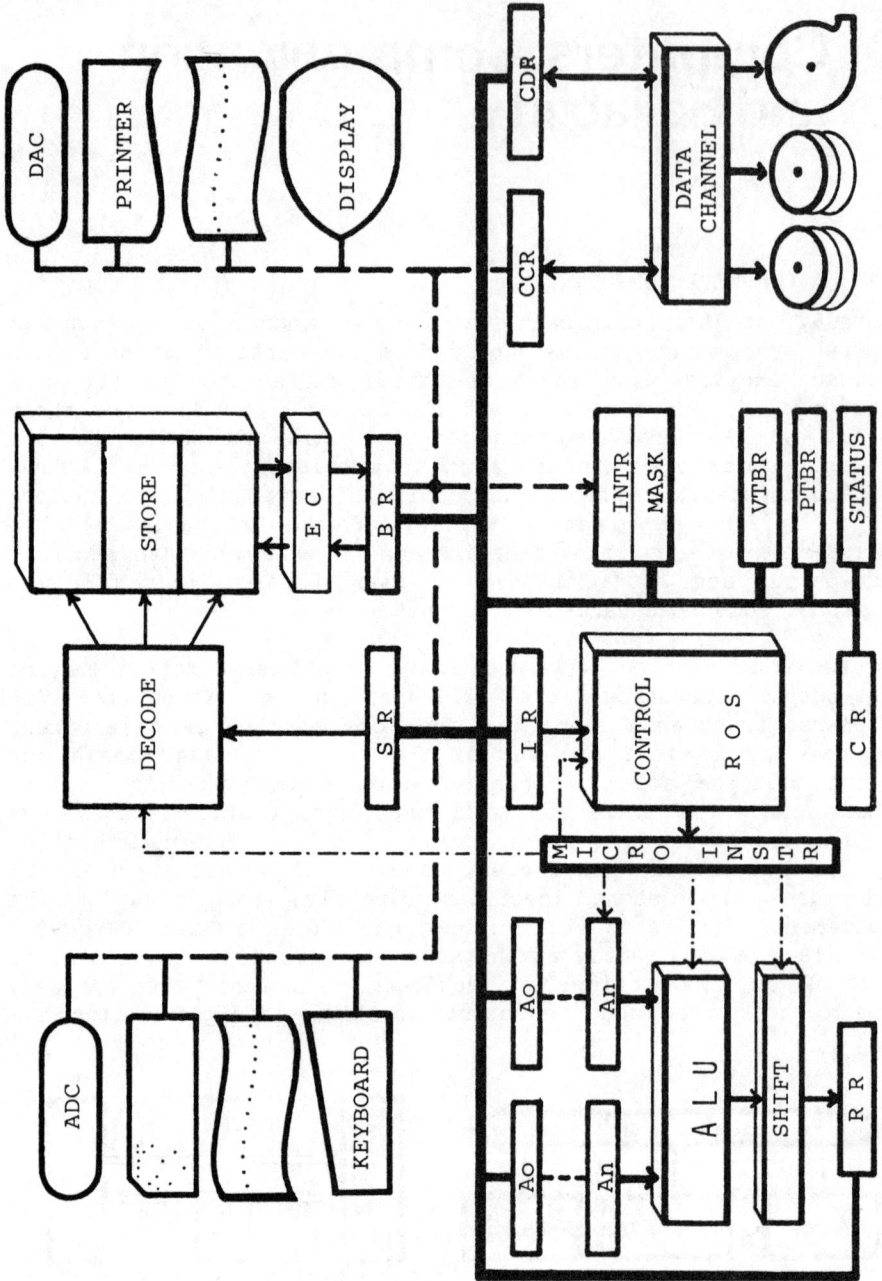

Note: EC is store error correcting logic.
Other units and registers are labelled as in the text.

FIG. 10.2 *A COMPLETE COMPUTER*

divided up so that some instructions are reserved for a "privileged" or system mode. This enables programs running in the ordinary mode to be kept under control by an operating system, since they can not tamper with such things as interrupts. An aid to keeping many programs, sharing the processor, under control is to add switched workspaces as well as two modes. A workspace contains everything which would have been in registers, yet can reside in store. Locations are reserved in the workspace for the essential registers, e.g. program counter and status, and a register is used to point to the current workspace. When a change between programs, or an interrupt, occurs it is only necessary to change a minimum number of registers and to switch workspaces. Many such small differences appear between the various computers on the market and are usually referred to collectively as the machines "architecture"

A complete machine is shown in Fig.10.2 which uses two busses and has been drawn schematically on the five block pattern. It contains all the major features of a typical small or mini-computer. It has a 16 bit word, which is almost universal. The store contains blocks of 16 thousand words of 750 ns. MOS, mixed with blocks of four thousand words of 250ns. bipolar, so that a small fast buffer can be arranged easily. The machine is bus-structured and is certainly micro-controlled. An optional writeable control store makes it micro-programmable as well. In the arithmetic and logic unit there would be eight general purpose registers, which serve as accumulators, index registers, etc. The usual logical and arithmetic instructions are included, as are a full set of floating point functions. These are all implemented by microcode. Very few small computers have a genuine D.S.A., normally only having a channel operating by single cycle-stealing. Disc drives and magnetic tape cassettes would operate with the channel, but to save expense the slower devices such as paper-tape and printer would have programmed transfer. A system clock and a flexible automatic priority interrupt system are included to allow real-time inputs from A-D converters. Outputs via D-A converters and to graphic visual displays must be included as well. If hardware stack handling and switched register sets are incorporated, the machine will be very fast in response to interrupts and easier to program. Also included to ease programming are multi-level indirect and indexed addressing structures. Paging hardware is now common on small machines, but segmentation is still unfortunately a rarity.

Obviously all of the points listed above will not be included in every model of computer in a range, but if they are not available as options there will be some applications for which the machine will not be suited.

10.2   DATA COMMUNICATION

Computers and terminals are regularly used at points remote from each other. The source and destination of data may be far apart. To cope with problems like these data must be communicated, often over large distances.

Simple connections for the transmission of data between two points may be unidirectional (simplex) or bidirectional with either concurrent (full duplex) or consecutive (half duplex) operation. Three types of line are available to connect the points: private, leased, or PSTN (public switched telephone network). The last two are controlled by national telecommunications companies (the Post Office in Great Britain). A leased line has some advantages over the PSTN. It is cheaper if the line usage is high, as a fixed rental is charged instead of the "per call" charge for the PSTN. The significant difference is that the connection over the switched network can go by many routes and so its characteristics change.

If signals are sent at the frequency at which they occur, without alteration, "base band" signalling is being employed. This can only be done over private wires of short (less than one kilometre) or medium (a few km) distances. A simple switching between two voltage levels representing zero and one will be inadequate for higher data rates, due to the effects of the resistance of the line and its capacitive coupling to earth. These act as a "filter" and cause attenuation of the voltage level of the signal until ultimately it disappears. Any transient pulse travelling along a line has its instantaneous current and voltage related by Ohm's law. This gives an apparent "characteristic impedance" for the line. If the pulse reaches the end of the line and finds a load which is not equal to this characteristic impedance, then something must happen to the voltage or current to retain the relationship. In fact a "reflection" is set up, which is a pulse of the excess current and voltage travelling back along the line. This disturbs the original pulse. If the transmission time between the source and the destination is small compared with the rise time of the transmitted signal, then the reflections can die away without upsetting the signal. As the data rate increases, the rise time decreases and the multiple reflections (reflections of the reflection!) seriously distort the signal.

The same argument applies at any discontinuity in the characteristics of the line, such as passing through a switch, and cables and paths with constant characteristics are sought. An example is a "twisted pair" cable which, if correctly terminated and driven by currents in opposite directions (differentially) in the two wires, is an acceptable solution for private wires. It can operate at quite high data rates and noise pickup is minimised by differential driving.

Leased lines and public lines can not be driven in the base band. Some form of "modulation", usually of a sine wave "carrier", is used to shift the data signal higher up in the frequency spectrum. The techniques used are similar to those for radio transmission, but the data is sent on wires. Three forms of analog modulation are possible:

AMPLITUDE MODULATION. The binary data is used to switch the carrier wave to one of two different amplitudes. Similar to A.M. radio, the system is susceptible to noise and is hardly ever used.

FREQUENCY MODULATION. The binary data is used to switch on one of two different carrier waves of different frequencies. One frequency represents a "1", the other a "0". This is the method used for all slow speed transmissions on the public network. A piece of equipment called a "modulator-demodulator" or "modem" is put at each end of the line to connect the terminal to the computer. The system is simple, reliable and cheap.

PHASE MODULATION. For higher speed transmisions a more complex system is used. This involves delaying the carrier by different amounts to represent patterns of data. Conceptually it may be thought of as switching between the carrier and a delayed copy of the carrier, for instance a sine wave and a cosine wave (90° delay). The phase-shift is detected at the receiving modem and is very unlikely to be distorted by any common electrical noise. At present it is used for all high speed transmission on PSTN and leased lines. As more modern telephone exchanges replace mechanical ones, digital modulation systems, particularly "pulse code modulation" will become more evident.

With large computer systems many terminals have to be connected. It is also common practice to connect a number of computers together to achieve a network which can give improved facilities. Multiple connection using terminals is illustrated in Fig.10.3. In a simple situation each connection requires its own pair of modems. For a large network this would be expensive and so line sharing is introduced. In a "multi-drop" connection all terminals share a line. Each message is prefixed with an address which only one terminal will recognise. That terminal accepts the line and all the others ignore it. However this does not give much security and two terminals can not transmit at the same instant. An improved arrangement is to give each logical connection its own physically seperate connection, even though the same wire is used to connect them. A "multiplexor" splits a single line up using either different frequencies (FDM, frequency division multiplexing) or seperate time intervals (TDM, time division multiplexing) for each of the separate terminals.

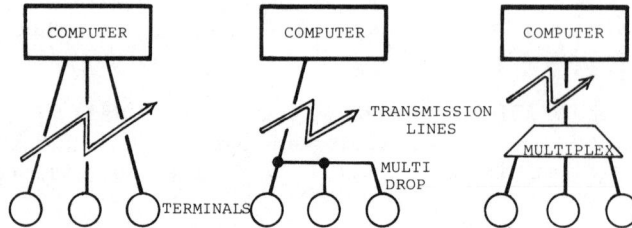

FIG. 10.3 MULTI-TERMINAL NETWORKS

10.3   RELIABILITY

Reliability is difficult to define, but high reliability is essential for the satisfactory operation of a computer. It may be considered as a measure of the ability of equipment to survive, without error, when in service. To be useful, a computer performing a million operations per second must be capable of correct operation for days or weeks (or hours at the very least). It is no comfort to know that it would work if only it did not fail every minute. A good idea of the reliability the public expects from computers can be gained by comparison with aeroplanes.

"If it flew, would *YOU* fly in it?"

Reliability must often be predicted. One can not build a computer and then expect to run it for five years before putting it on the market just to see how reliable it is. The total reliability of a machine depends on the failure rates of the individual components. These are found by testing large numbers of each component under extreme conditions of temperature, environment and current load (rating). These standard figures, supported by feedback from previous products, can be used to make predictions. Factors are introduced to allow for deviations in temperature (standard is 10-20°C), environment (office) and rating.

The failure rate for the machine is defined as the decrease in operative components from the total number. Assumptions are then made: all components have constant failure rates; failure rates of various components are independent; and all components must function for the machine to function.

The total failure rate "F" is the sum of all the individual failure rates, adjusted by the factors mentioned before. The result is the probability that the machine is operational, say 0.97, and is fairly meaningless. Of more use is the inverse of the system failure rate, which is the "mean time between failure" (MTBF), the average time the machine will run between faults.

$$\text{Total failure rate } F = \frac{\frac{-dN}{dt}}{N} \qquad \text{Reliability } R = e^{-Ft} = e^{-t/MTBF}$$

Typical minicomputers have MTBFs of 6 months to a year. Typical component failure rates are .001% per thousand hours for a small integrated circuit, .02% per thousand hours for a micro-processor, and even .0001% per thousand hours for a connection between two wires!

The theoretical reliability is no guarantee of an operational system, because each failure will take time to repair. The "availability" or "uptime ratio" is calculated from the MTBF and the MTRF, the mean time to repair a failure.

$$\text{AVAILABILITY} = MTBF/(MTBF+MTRF)$$

It is apparent that halving the MTRF will increase availability by the same amount as doubling the MTBF. Hence the systems "maintainability" is most important and warrants much design time being spent to make fault finding simple. If an extremely reliable machine is needed, redundant hardware must be included to take over if a failure occurs.

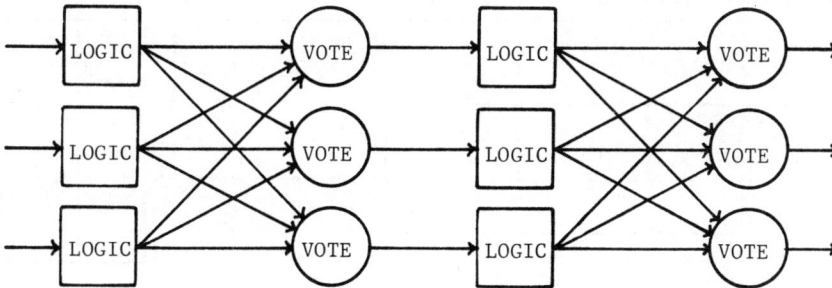

FIG. 10.4 *TRIPLE MODULAR REDUNDANCY*

An example of a "fault tolerant" system uses triple modular redundancy (TMR), shown in Fig.10.4. Each part of the system is triplicated, any one wrong answer being statically masked out by the other two correct answers. A voting circuit is used to compare the output of three identical modules and the majority decision prevails. Obviously the voter could fail, as could the connections, so they are all triplicated. Once a module has been identified as faulty it could be removed, or switched out, to be replaced by a new or stand-by module. The system functions all the while as two modules still agree at that point. This is an expensive solution and in an ordinary business or scientific environment improvement in reliability could be achieved by adding redundant information instead of redundant hardware. Obviously it does not matter if a given bit of information is in error if it is known that an error has occurred and the program can be run again, or provided it is known where the error occurred. The use of redundant codes to permit error detection (and even correction) is common practice in modern computers.

The simplest error detector is the "parity bit". A character or word has the number of ones or zeros counted. An extra bit is added to ensure that an odd or even number then exists. If the counting is done again and compared with the check, any single (or odd number) of bits in error is signified. A procedure which makes the number of bits in the complete word or character, including the check, odd or even is called odd or even parity accordingly. For example, the seven bit ASCII character code normally has an eighth bit added to give even parity counting the ones.

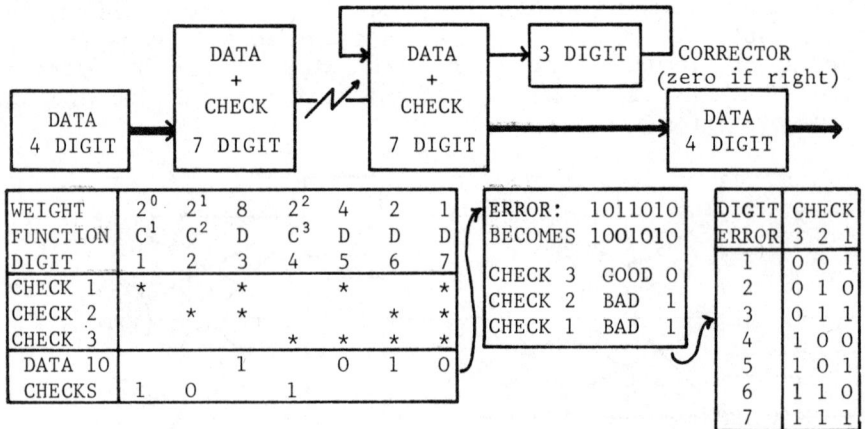

```
                          ┌──────────────────────────┐
  ┌──────────┐   ┌──────────┐   ┌──────────┐  ┌──────────┐
  │          │   │  DATA    │   │  DATA    │  │ 3 DIGIT  │  CORRECTOR
  │          │   │   +      │   │   +      │  └──────────┘  (zero if right)
  │  DATA    │→  │  CHECK   │~~→│  CHECK   │→              ┌──────────┐
  │ 4 DIGIT  │   │ 7 DIGIT  │   │ 7 DIGIT  │               │  DATA    │→
  └──────────┘   └──────────┘   └──────────┘               │ 4 DIGIT  │
                                                            └──────────┘
```

WEIGHT	2^0	2^1	8	2^2	4	2	1
FUNCTION	c^1	c^2	D	c^3	D	D	D
DIGIT	1	2	3	4	5	6	7
CHECK 1	*		*		*		*
CHECK 2		*	*			*	*
CHECK 3				*	*	*	*
DATA 10			1		0	1	0
CHECKS	1	0		1			

ERROR:	1011010	
BECOMES	1001010	
CHECK 3	GOOD	0
CHECK 2	BAD	1
CHECK 1	BAD	1

DIGIT ERROR	CHECK 3 2 1
1	0 0 1
2	0 1 0
3	0 1 1
4	1 0 0
5	1 0 1
6	1 1 0
7	1 1 1

FIG. 10.5 *HAMMING CODE ERROR CORRECTION*

If more check bits are used an error can be not only detected, but also corrected, as its position in the word can be located. An example of this type of "error correcting" code, which is now commonly used for minicomputer stores is, the "Hamming" code. Each check digit checks a selection of the bits in a word by even parity. The check digits are distributed throughout the word such that they do not check on each other. The selection of data bits for each check is based on the binary pattern. The first check is on all positions, the binary code of which contains the least significant bit. The second check is on all positions with the second bit in the corresponding binary code, and so on. When checks are performed, the hardware finds the intersection of checks indicating error and this determines the position in error. The check has "c" bits and so can indicate correct (all zero checks) or 2^c-1 intersections, or positions in error. This number must include the check bits themselves, as they are just as likely to fail. An example using a four bit word (binary 1010) is shown in Fig.10.5. Three check bits are required, which seems inefficient, but for a 16 bit word only 5 check bits are needed.

Such a code may be made double error detecting as well as single error correcting if an extra even parity check is added to cover all the bits including the checks. A single error is shown up by the new overall parity and is located as in the example. A double error gives correct overall parity, but shows incorrect in the "Hamming" check. If both overall and all individual checks are zero there is no error. With a normal 16 bit computer word, 22 bits are stored to give this level of protection.

The most obvious way to obtain a reliable system is to design with reliability in mind from the start. A common design problem serves as an example. Shaft encoders are intended to output a binary number which represents the position of rotation of a shaft. A disc with binary pattern in light and dark paint, and a photoelectric cell could be used. This would give transient errors repeatedly as the disc rotated, if ordinary binary code were used. Passing from 3 (011) to 4 (100), there would be an instant when both showed and 111 (7) would appear as the output. The use of the "Gray" code from the outset removes the problem. It changes in one position only, when incrementing from one code to the next, and so can only be inaccurate by one increment.

GRAY:	0000 0001 0011 0010 0110 0111 0101 0100	
BINARY:	0000 0001 0010 0011 0100 0101 0110 0111	
GRAY:	1100 1101 1111 1110 1010 1011 1001 1000	
BINARY:	1000 1001 1010 1011 1100 1101 1110 1111	etc.

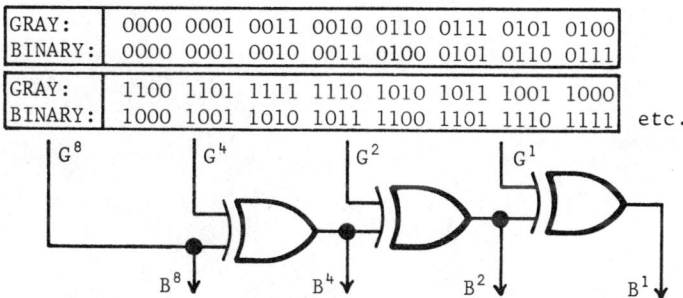

FIG. 10.6 GRAY TO BINARY CODE CONVERSION

The Gray code would also be very suitable for the micro-program address counter. No transients could occur, as the address steps for the following micro-instruction fetch. A Gray code up/down counter would be ideal for this purpose and, if designed into the machine from the very start, could prevent possible unreliability in service.

11 Construction and Implementation

11.1   LOGIC ELEMENTS

All the processing, control and interface logic has been described on the assumption that gates and registers can be fabricated somehow. One could use any form of implementation, for instance relays or thermionic valves, as were used in the earliest of computers built during the 1940s. A relay gate operates when its coil is energised, thus closing its output contact(s). If two contacts are placed in series or parallel and are connected between following coils and their energising power source, then logical functions may be performed. Fig. 11.1 shows AND and OR gates operating on this principle.

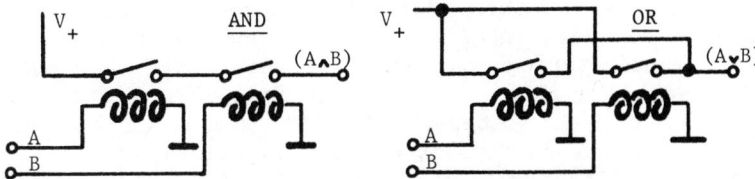

FIG. 11.1 RELAY GATE IMPLEMENTATION

The operation of such gates is very easy to understand, but there are three insurmountable problems. The contacts of the switches are unreliable, as are all mechanical devices, the power necessary to energise the coils is large, and the switching speed is quite slow. Conceptually the same, modern integrated circuit logic implementations use transistors as the switches.

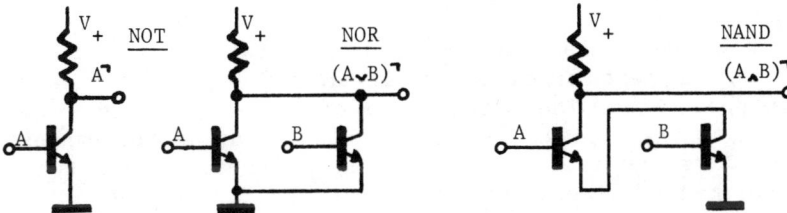

FIG. 11.2 TRANSISTOR INVERTER AND GATES

A transistor connects its "emitter" to its "collector" by a high resistance if the voltage on its "base" is low (below 0.8V above the emitter voltage). A transistor connects its emitter to its collector by a low resistance if the voltage on its base is high (above 2V above the emitter voltage). Hence the circuit in Fig. 11.2 shows a simple transistor inverter. A similar arrangement works for MOS transistors, though by an entirely different internal process. To produce gates, an analogy to the relay implementation can be used, but NAND and NOR forms will be produced due to the inherent inversion of a transistor mentioned above.

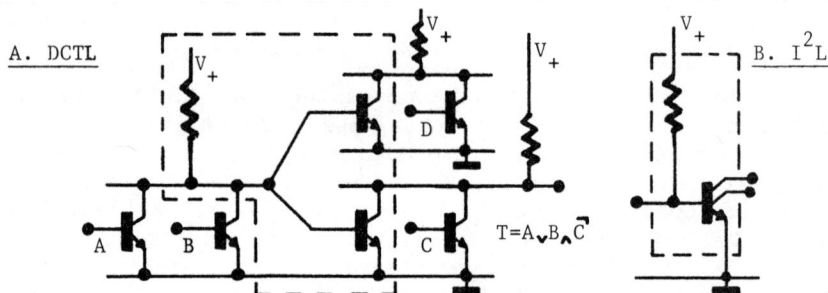

FIG. 11.3 *DIRECT COUPLED TRANSISTOR LOGIC*

The problem with this "direct coupled transistor logic" approach was that if many gates were connected together, then, due to the manufacturing tolerances of the components, one input transistor would "hog" all the current from the output to which it was connected, and other transistors connected to the same output might not get sufficient current to switch over. A further drawback was that the voltage required for "A" and "B" inputs to the NAND gate were different, with the "A" input requiring a higher voltage to switch, thus giving a narrower separation between zero and one logic levels. Many approaches were explored to overcome these problems, involving quite complex circuits whose operations are more difficult to visualise. The most common of these types of logic is transistor transistor logic or T^2L. There is a vast array of books, pamphlets and data sheets devoted to it, and it was once the most prevalent form of implementation.

Recently there has been renewed interest in the DCTL form because of a neat trick which is available due to integrated circuit production. The dotted area of the circuit in Fig. 11.3 gave rise to the problem because of manufacturing tolerances. If, instead of making each basic part as one gate, as was done with T^2L, one made the critical tolerance parts on one integrated circuit, then there would be no tolerance difference and the problem would be solved, giving a far simpler manufacturing process. This form of logic is called Integrated Injection Logic or I^2L and a basic circuit element, the dotted area referred to, is shown at the bottom of Fig. 11.5. The second transistor is included to give more uniform current supply to the switching transistors and, as can be seen, parts of the switching transistors are connected in parallel, so they must act together and can be "integrated" into one.

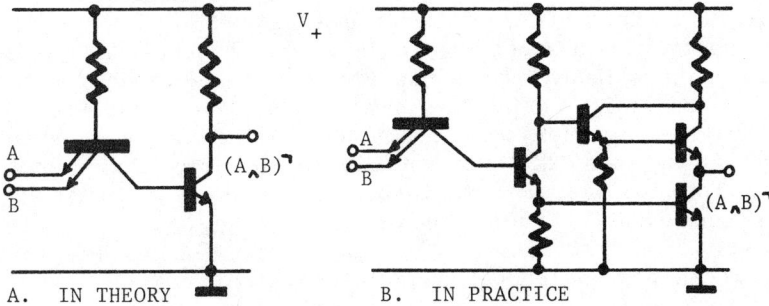

A.   IN THEORY   B.   IN PRACTICE

FIG. 11.4 TRANSISTOR TRANSISTOR LOGIC

The speed-power product mentioned in Chapter 8 is just as important in the implementation of the logic circuits of a machine as in the store. Typical T^2L logic gates have a speed-power product of 50 picojoules, with a propagation delay of 10-20 nanoseconds. The fastest form of logic used in modern computers is "emitter coupled logic" with a speed-power product of 100 picojoules, but a propagation delay of only 1-3 nanoseconds. With integrated injection logic, the saving due to high packing density (200 gates per square millimetre) is augmented by the extremely low speed-power product, of approximately 0.5 picojoule. The propogation delay for I^2L is about 20-50 nanoseconds. These figures can be compared with the theoretical limit of 0.001 picojoule and with the values found by measurement of a "neuron". This basic brain cell has a speed-power product of less than 0.1 picojoule, but a propagation delay of 100 microseconds, making I^2L nearly comparable!

11.2   INTEGRATED CIRCUIT PRODUCTION

The production of integrated circuits is central to the success of modern mini-computers. The complete process for production of an integrated circuit, the I^2L basic unit described above, is shown in Fig. 11.5. There are other production processes, but the basic concepts are similar. Computers are constructed from common chemical elements, silicon being the second most common on earth (sand is mainly SiO_2).

A pure piece of silicon has a full outer shell of electrons; as there are no free spaces or spare electrons, it does not conduct electricity well. However, if we add small amounts of impurities, with very close structures but with one more or one less electron in the outer shell, then the material will start to conduct a little and is called a "semi-conductor". If one adds an impurity with an extra electron in its outer shell, it is a "donor" of electrons with negative charge and is called "N-type". If an impurity with one electron less than silicon in its outer shell, then it is an "acceptor" of electrons and is "P-type", as it has extra positively charged "holes" or an absence of electrons. Transistors are made from a sandwich of three layers, either PNP or, more commonly, NPN. The symbol for the transistor has an arrow on the emitter to label the direction of conventional current flow, into PNP type or out of NPN type. The production process for individual transistors is similar to that for the simple integrated circuit and for circuits with many tens of thousands of transistors, as in large computer circuits, micro-processors and pocket calculators.

The silicon is sliced into "wafers" approximately two inches in diameter and a layer of monocrystalline silicon is deposited onto them to give uniform properties to the surface, where the circuit will be made. The choice of impurities comes from a study of the periodic table of elements and their chemical properties. For silicon, the donor impurity is phosphorus and the acceptor impurity is boron. Transistors are also made using germanium as the base material or "substrate" and the impurities are aluminium as an acceptor and arsenic as a donor! However, the properties of silicon transistors are more suited to high speed digital circuits and silicon is almost universal in integrated circuits.

The next stage in the process is to arrange the impurities in the amounts required, in the positions required on the wafer. The depth of diffusion of the impurities into the silicon, and their concentration, depends on the time of exposure to the vapour containing the impurity and the temperature. To determine the position on the wafer, a masking process must be used to stop the impurity penetrating, where it is not required.

The pure silicon has a layer of silicon dioxide produced by oxidising its surface. This is reasonably inert and provides a barrier through which the impurities will not pass. It is then coated with a layer of liquid plastic, called "photo-resist", which reacts to ultra-violet light by polymerising and solidifying. It is also resistant to an acid, which can etch away the silicon dioxide. A mask is prepared photographically, the same size as the wafer but produced from a master many feet square to get the intricate detail, with dimensions as small as 10^{-9}m, required for the tiny integrated circuit. The plastic layer is exposed to ultra-violet light through the mask and

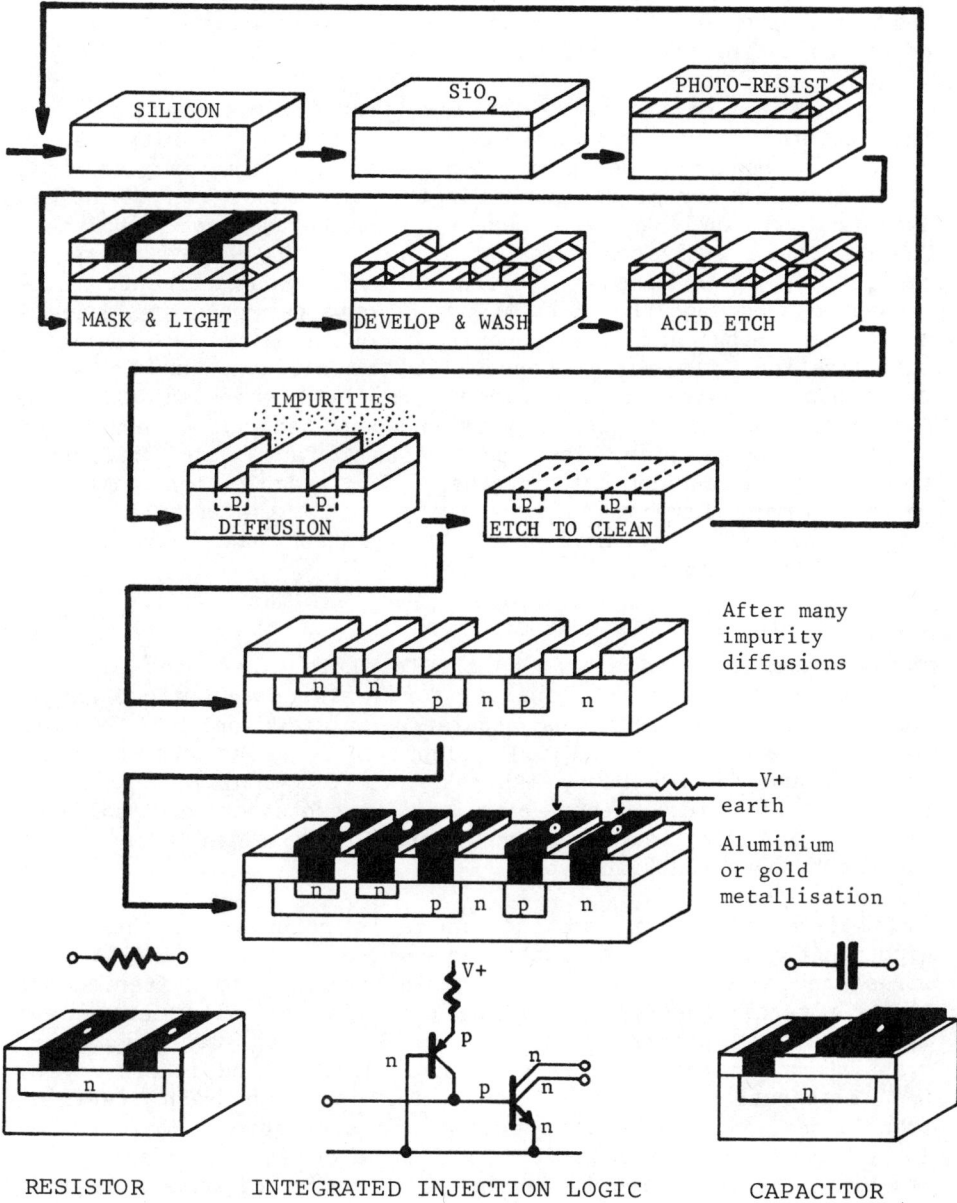

FIG. 11.5 *INTEGRATED CIRCUIT PRODUCTION*

hardens where the light falls on it. The remainder may be removed and then the silicon dioxide etched away where it is not protected by the photo-resist.

The position on the wafer for the first impurity diffusion is thus determined and adequate exposure to the impurity vapour gives the required depth of impurity. The remaining silicon dioxide, which formed the mask for the diffusion, can be etched away and the whole process repeated to add further impurities. The result is a silicon wafer with many depths and positions of impurities, some inside others, forming the circuit. The connections between the circuit and the outside world are made by a further mask and the deposition of a gold or aluminium metallisation film which connects to the silicon, and to which wires can be soldered. The circuit is then connected via these microscopic wires to pins and is encapsulated in a ceramic or plastic package for its protection. Parts of different transistors which connect together, for example the base and emitter N-type in Fig. 11.5, are physically the same piece of N-type silicon. They have been "integrated" and this is the explanation of the name.

11.3   CONSTRUCTION AND CONNECTION

The most common package type is the "dual in line" package. This consists of a plastic or ceramic (for a wider temperature range) encapsulation. Two pin rows separated by 0.3" or 0.6" contain 7,8,12 or 20 pins on an 0.1" pitch. This gives the standard 14,16,24 and 40 pin DILs, though other pin configurations are possible. The pins either plug into sockets or are soldered directly and the low cost and ease of installation make this package type very attractive.

The final stage of construction is to connect the integrated circuits together. As was mentioned earlier, distance = delay, so wires need to be as short as possible. Reliability criterion and miniaturisation have provided the pressure to build larger and larger scale integrated circuits (LSI), with more and more transistors connected by the mask metallisation and inherently by the integration. A unit containing ten thousand separate transistors, each with its package and connections, takes up a lot of space, can have faults in connection and is slow due to its size. The same circuit can now be constructed on a half inch square of silicon.

The cost of an LSI circuit is dominated by its area, hence the more gates that can be packed into a given size of chip, the cheaper each gate element will be. The desirability of logic implementations such as MOS and I^2L is obvious.

It is necessary to incorporate some extra components, for power smoothing and to connect to the outside world, and it is normal to mount the integrated circuits and other components on printed circuit boards (PCBs). An epoxy glass (like fibreglass) board has a layer of copper deposited on either side of it. By a similar photo-masking process, followed by etching, copper is removed to leave the connections required. If the two layers of connection are not sufficient, then multi-layer boards are used where a number of boards, made as described, are bonded together. The components are soldered onto the copper, connecting pads being left specially for this.

The processes described are all automated and once a unit has been produced, replicas can be churned out. The majority of the cost is in the design and layout of PCBs, and design and layout of integrated circuit masks, and this means that, whilst the first unit is very expensive, subsequent units are cheap. This accounts for the explosion in sales of digital watches, pocket calculators and computers.

Appendix A
Electrical and Logical Symbols

The use of electrical symbols has been kept to a minimum, but those which were unavoidable are shown below.

Computer logic symbols have undergone many metamorphoses, as international standards were proposed, tried and changed. Those used in this book are based on the American military standard 806B, which is almost universal in small computer descriptions. The revised British standard is so similar that this usage represents common industrial practice. Where symbols are not defined, the general logic "box" approach (also common practice) has been adopted to improve clarity.

In expressions: ∧ AND, ∨ OR, ⌐ NOT, + PLUS, . MULTIPLY

NO CONNECTION	CONNECTION	RESISTOR	CAPACITOR	TRANSISTOR	COIL

INVERTER	AND	OR	NAND	NOR	EXCLUSIVE OR

BISTABLES	DELAY	REGISTER

1/2 ADDER	FULL ADDER	ANY GENERAL LOGIC

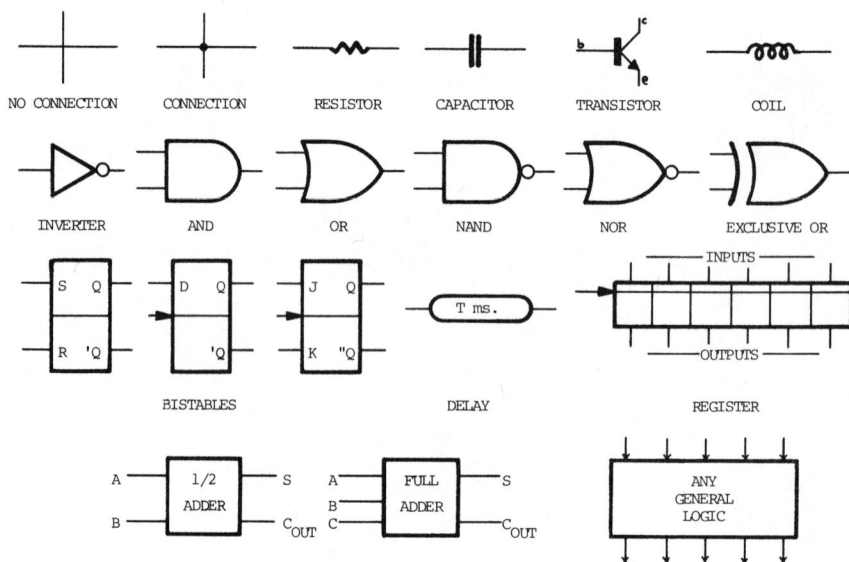

FIG. A.1 ELECTRICAL AND LOGICAL SYMBOLS

An extra convention has been adopted in the drawings of the bus highway structure. Only the first and last units are shown to represent the multi-wire bus and multiple sets of gates.

Appendix B
Glossary of Terms

The "jargon" used in computing is probably no worse than in any other technological area, but it is sometimes awkward, as words which have regular meanings in the English language are occasionally used as jargon terms with subtle differences in meaning. An attempt has been made to keep such usage to a minimum, and to be consistent, but some terms can not be avoided, and a glossary of them and their usual definitions follows.

ACCUMULATOR: A register used to accumulate partial results, and to hold data which is being operated on. This is one use of a general purpose register.

ADDEND, AUGEND: The two numbers added together by the addition operation are called the addend and the augend.

BINARY: A number representation system which uses only two digits (0 & 1), and in which the columns represent ones, twos, fours and eights, etc. in a similar fashion to decimal ones, tens and hundreds.
E.G. 10=2   11=3   101=5   1110=14   1000101=69.

BISTABLE: A device capable of remaining in one of two stable "states". It can be switched from one to another and so can hold the value of 1 binary digit over a period of time.

BIT: A single binary digit (0 or 1) is called a bit. A group of eight bits is called a BYTE, and a group of 16 bits (up to 60 bits) forms a computer WORD. A bistable stores a single bit.

BRANCH (JUMP): Alterations to the sequence of instructions being performed are made using a branch instruction. The next instruction is not taken from the next location, but from the location given by the branch. Conditional branch instructions perform the branch only if some specified criteria is met, e.g. + - zero. Subroutine branch instructions alter the instruction flow, but also store the previous content of the program counter so that the original sequence can be re-joined.

BUS, BUS HIGHWAY: A bus is a collection of wires (from the electrical supply "busbar") and a bus highway is a group of wires forming a complete connection between many units, peripherals or registers.

CAPACITY: Either the size of a disc or store, in bits, bytes or words, <u>or</u> the maximum data transfer rate to extract or store data in the store.

CARRY: If two numbers are added together as digit pairs, then a carry may be produced, which has to be added in with the next digit pair. In binary addition this is simple, as the only carries which can be produced are 0 and 1.

CARRY PREDICTION: Normally digit pairs are added and the result examined to see if there was a carry (which would be added into the next stage). It is easier to examine the input numbers and determine whether there will be a carry *INTO* any stage, thus completing the calculation in a fraction of time.

CLOCK: A regular sequence of 0,1,0,1, etc. (pulses) which is used to control the timing and synchronise separate actions in a machine.

COMPLEMENT: The one's complement is found by changing all zeros into ones and vice versa. This is also the "inverse" and for a single bit (or flag) 0:=1 and 1:=0. This does not represent a true negative, but if 1 is added in the least significant position of a one's complement number, the two's complement is formed, which gives the "negative" number.

DATA: Information used by a program, which is not normally part of the program's sequence of instructions is called data, e.g. numbers to be added, characters to be printed.

EXECUTE: The half of the main computer cycle where an instruction is obeyed and the desired operation(s) happen.

EXPONENT: A real number consists of two parts, a mantissa and an exponent. The mantissa represents the value of the significant digits of the number, wheras the exponent represents the scaling factor which gives the correct position for the decimal (binary) point.

$0.0285 = 2.85 \times 10^{-2}$ Mantissa 2.85, Exponent -2.

$13824 = 1.10110 \times 2^{1101}$ Mantissa 1.1011 ($= 27/16$), Exponent 1101 ($= 8192$).

FALSE: A condition (or flag) false implies something will not happen, gates are not enabled, or a bit is zero, with the normal convention.

FETCH: The first half of a main machine cycle, when an instruction is fetched from store, prior to being executed.

FIRMWARE: Those parts of a computer's control which are not electronics, but are sequences of instructions or micro-instructions, and yet are fixed and do not change for each new program. Firmware is an extension of hardware whereby some program sequences are considered to be an integral part of the machine.

FLOATING POINT: A real number having exponent and mantissa is called a floating point number. This representation is used to extend the useful range of numbers which can be held in a given size of machine word.

GATE: An electronic circuit which performs one of the logical operations AND, NAND, OR, NOR, EXCLUSIVE OR, on its inputs, to give a true or false (1 or 0) output.

HARDWARE: The electronic circuits and mechanical parts which make up into a computer are called hardware. This is distinguished from the sequences of instructions (software) which set the hardware up to perform the required steps.

HEXADECIMAL: A number representation system which has digits 0-9 and A-F, with columns for ones, sixteens, and two hundred and fifty sixes, instead of the decimal 1, 10s, and 100s.

INSTRUCTION: A coded command which sets the hardware so that it performs a desired operation, possibly using the arithmetic and logic unit, input-output section, or store.

INTEGER: A whole number having only a given magnitude and a sign (+ or -), with no scaling, decimal (binary) point, or fractional part.

LATENCY: The average access time to a cyclic store, such as a disc, where the access time varies due to the length of rotation before the correct bits appear.

LOGIC LEVELS: The voltages used to represent true (1) and false (0) within the computer.

MANTISSA: The magnitude part (significant digits) of a floating point number. This is described more fully under "exponent".

MEMORY: A device in which data can be accessed by its content or form and in which a knowledge of the location of an item is unnecessary for it to be recovered. Found only in small units as "associative store", or "Content Addressable Memory", but not common in computers yet. Manufacturers sometimes mistakenly use this term for STORE.

MULTIPLICAND, MULTIPLIER: The two numbers which are multiplied together by multiplier logic to give a result. Multiplicand times multiplier gives result.

NORMALISE: A number is normalised when it is arranged so that the maximum number of significant digits are held and there are no leading zeros following the decimal point. A similar criterion applies for binary normalised numbers. 0.00057 is not normalised, whereas 0.57201 is.

OPERAND: Data which can be operated on or used as input for addition, multiplication, shifting, etc. It may represent a number, characters, flags, or an address.

OPERATOR: A function which is to be performed on or between operands. It may be arithmetic or logical; some examples are add, divide, exclusive or, and shift.

PERMANENT: A store is said to be permanent if it will retain the data set into it indefinitely, if all power is removed from it. Core stores are permanent, whereas IC stores are not.

PROGRAM (STORED): A sequence of instructions which if performed will produce answers or actions previously decided on by the programmer. Can be in machine language (ADD, CMA, mnemonic form), or in high level languages, with pidgin-english-like form, but uniquely interpretable structure and grammar.

RESET: Same as "clear", set to zero, opposite of "set" for a bistable or register.

ROTATE: A computer word is rotated when it is moved a place or places to right or left and bits which come off one end are put back in at the other.

SHIFT: A computer word is shifted when it is moved a place or places to right or left and bits which come off one end are lost. Defined bits are fed in to fill the gaps; they are normally zeros at the least significant end and duplicates of the most significant bit at the other end.

STATE: A machine or any part of it is said to be in a certain "state" at a given time and this defines its condition completely, with all the voltages, contents of any store, etc. A single bistable can exist in one of two states, set or reset, and so sits in the 0-state or the 1-state.

STORE: That part of a computer which holds all the instructions and data required to run a given program. Any electronic mechanism which can hold "states" over time (and so store data) and can retrieve the information only if it is given the location at which it was stored may be termed a store.

TRUE: The condition (or a flag) true implies that something will happen, gates are enabled, or that a bit is a one.

TRUTH TABLE: A complete description of the action of a logic circuit (combinatorial) is given by all possible input combinations and the outputs corresponding to them. This is written down in 1s and 0s, and is called a truth table.

VOLATILE: Describes a store, the content of which is lost if power is removed from the system. Opposite of permanent.

WORD: A group of bits, handled in the computer as a single unit, is called a word. There are two types of word, instruction words, containing commands which are parts of a program, and data words, containing numbers, characters, etc. which are used during execution of a program.

Appendix C
Summary of Peripheral Characteristics

C.1 PUNCHED PAPER TAPE

15-1000 ch/sec read, 10-300 ch/s punch, 10-1000 feet/reel.

Punched 8 hole paper or mylar tape one inch wide, coded in ASCII, a cheap and common form of I/O for small computers. Tape is fed mechanically by pinch-roller, or by the small sprocket holes in the tape; reading is done by light and photo-electric sensors, and punching by electro-mechanical solenoids. 5, 6 and 7 hole tape, with narrower paper and different coding, are also found.

C.2 PUNCHED CARDS

250-1200 cpm read, 100-300 cpm punch, 250-3500 card hopper.

Cards of 80 columns, 12 rows, with rectangular holes, or 96 columns, 8 rows, with round holes, fed one at a time. Reading and punching mechanisms similar to paper tape; off-line card punching equipment is cheap, common and simple to use.

C.3 KEYBOARD

10-45ch/sec, 7 bit ASCII code character per key.

Standard 44 key alphanumeric keyboard, often augmented to 65 keys including control codes, with photo-electrical or electro-mechanical sensing, generates 7-8 bit parallel codes. For control by operators, text input and interactive operation.

C.4 SERIAL PRINTER

10-45 ch/s, (to 250 ch/s), continuous paper 8-13" wide.

Printed page, character at a time, electromechanical impact, or non-impact (xeronic, ink jet or thermal) printing, possibly needing special paper. Paper fed by pinched roller, or platen feed, mechanically. Slow, but useful as an interactive terminal (with keyboard), console, or small system printer.

C.5 LINE PRINTER

300-2000 lpm, 60-160 ch/line, continuous paper 13" (to 24") wide.

Printed page, line at a time, using buffer. Same methods of printing as slow printers, but usually impact from a chain or train of mirror image characters. Paper feed by sprocket drive meshing with holes in paper, but handling problems at the higher speeds. Expensive but fast output of all printed information.

C.6   VISUAL DISPLAY UNIT

10 ch/s-50K ch/s, 300-4000 characters on screen at a time.

Uses a cathode ray tube; an electron beam writes characters and graphic data onto a phosphor screen. Refreshed screen type, or storage tube using flood beams to hold charge pattern on screen; used for interactive, computer aided design (CAD), and monitoring systems to present transient data quickly.

C.7   MAGNETIC TAPE CASSETTE

100-60K ch/s, 800-1600 bits/inch, 150-600 feet/cassette.

Magnetic ferric oxide coating on plastic tape, either in Phillips type cassette (1 track per side, 1/8" wide tape) or, less commonly in larger cartridges (2 tracks per side, 1/4" wide tape). Fixed read-write head senses or induces magnetisation in the surface layer on the tape as it is moved past the head. Very convenient and cheap store for small/medium data volumes, often included in terminals as the modern replacement for paper tape.

C.8   MAGNETIC TAPE, INDUSTRY COMPATIBLE

10K-1.5M ch/s, 200-6250 bits/inch, 1200-3600 feet on 10" reel.

Magnetic coated plastic tape 1/2" wide, with 7 or 9 tracks across the tape. Stationary read-write heads, tape moved over them, in contact, by pinched roller, from vacuum buffer columns to give low inertia. One character read/written at an instant, but data normally blocked up, with inter-record gaps for stop and start of tape. Can be used for long-term storage of large amounts of data.

C.9   MAGNETIC DISC, FIXED HEAD

0.1-2.5M ch/s, 0.1-10M chars stored, 5-20 msec access time.

Aluminium alloy disc with magnetic coated surface is rotated continuously past fixed read-write heads, not touching the surface and not removable. One head per track of data. High speed backing store used for system, paging, etc. but expensive for the volume it provides.

C.10   MAGNETIC DISC, MOVING HEAD

0.1-1.0M ch/s, 2-400M chars stored, 20-100 msec access time.

Only one read-write head per surface, but often many (10-20) surfaces. Head moved to correct track by linear motor, under control of mechanical detent or servo tracks on reserved surface of disc. Often in form of disc-packs which can be removed, providing a large, cheap and fast data store.

C.11   DIGITAL TO ANALOG CONVERTER (D/A)

0.5-20 microsec/word converted, resolution 8-16 bits/value.

A digital word is converted to a voltage (usually in range $\pm$10v.) and output to perform some control function. Conversion uses a "ladder" network of resistors, R, R/2, R/4, etc. connected to a voltage source and the bits switch in the correct parts of the ladder to give the right voltage. All electronic, sometimes one converter is multiplexed to a few outputs.

C.12   ANALOG TO DIGITAL CONVERTER (A/D)

5-2000 microsec/word converted, resolution 8-16 bits/value.

Analog voltages are converted to the nearest digital value by comparison of input voltage with output of a D/A converter. The value to the D/A is altered continuously or by successive approximation (repeated halving) until values are equal. The value being put to the D/A is then the digital equivalent of the analog input. All electronic and one converter is commonly multiplexed, or time-shared, amongst a number of inputs.

C.13   DIRECT DIGITAL INPUT-OUTPUT

Machine speed 1-100M ch/s, machine word at a time.

Input from digital sensors, external logic, switches, etc. output to lamps, digital control lines, online computer control systems, to open or shut valves, etc. Operation performed by the data is usually very much slower than the possible input-output rate.

C.14   SHAFT POSITION ENCODER

5-500 rev/min, 6-16 bit digital code input.

Really a subset of C.13, giving direct indication of shaft rotation or position for computer control. 6-16 bits parallel input in "Gray" code, or other reflected code, where only one bit is changed at a time (like K-map coding). Sensing is done by photo-electric or brush and disc sensors, hence special Gray code to avoid ambiguity between adjacent values as the shaft moves.

Appendix D
Speed and Conversion Tables

D.1   SPEED TABLE

A table of speeds for peripherals follows. This compares the standard numbers of changes per second on a transmission line (baud) with the normal measures of data transfer rate. The baud rate can, in simple transmission systems, be approximated to the bits per second, though this is not strictly accurate.

BAUD bps	ASYNC# cps*	SYNCH# cps*	WORDS wpm*	CARDS cpm*	LINES lpm*
110	10	-	100	7	6
150	15	-	150	9	8
300	30	-	300	19	17
600	60	-	600	38	34
1200	120	150	1500	86	70
2400	240	300	3000	170	140
4800	480	600	6000	340	275
9600	960	1200	12000	680	550
40800	4080	5100	51000	2910	2350
48000	4800	6000	60000	3400	2750

Asynchronous transmission of characters uses 10 or 11 bits per character and synchronous transmission uses 8 bits per character, filling blank time with SYN characters.

* cps Characters per second including start/stop bits.

* wpm Words per minute, average 6 character words.

* cpm Cards per minute, 80 column cards, 2/3 full and trailing spaces compressed above 600 baud.

* lpm Lines per minute, 132 column lines, 2/3 full.

D.2   ASCII CHARACTER CODING

The American Standard Code for Information Interchange, which is almost identical to the European and British standard data codes, uses the all zero bit code as a NULL character and the all ones code as a DELete or rub-out character. Codes from hexadecimal 01 to 1F are control characters with the following definitions:

HEX	NAME	DEFINITION	HEX	NAME	DEFINITION
00	NUL	Null	10	DLE	Data link escape
01	SOH	Start of header	11	DC1	Reader on
02	STX	Start of text	12	DC2	Tape (aux) on
03	ETX	End of text	13	DC3	Reader off
04	EOT	End transmission	14	DC4	Tape (aux) off
05	ENQ	Enquire, who R U	15	NAK	Not acknowledge
06	ACK	Acknowledge	16	SYN	Synchronous idle
07	BEL	Ring bell	17	ETB	End of text block
08	BS	Backspace	18	CAN	Cancel
09	HT	Horizontal tab	19	EM	End of medium
0A	LF	Line feed	1A	SUB	Substitute
0B	VT	Vertical tab	1B	ESC	Escape
0C	FF	Form feed	1C	FS	File seperator
0D	CR	Carriage return	1D	GS	Group seperator
0E	SO	Shift out	1E	RS	Record seperator
0F	SI	Shift in	1F	US	Unit seperator

Codes from 11-14 are used to control auxiliary paper or magnetic cassette tape units and graphic terminals use 1C-1F to select the modes for vector drawing. The remaining codes provide a space character (20) and 94 printable characters listed below.

HEX	CH	HEX	CH	HEX	CH	HEX	CH	HEX	CH	HEX	CH
		30	0	40	@	50	P	60	`	70	p
21	!	31	1	41	A	51	Q	61	a	71	q
22	"	32	2	42	B	52	R	62	b	72	r
23	#	33	3	43	C	53	S	63	c	73	s
24	$	34	4	44	D	54	T	64	d	74	t
25	%	35	5	45	E	55	U	65	e	75	u
26	&	36	6	46	F	56	V	66	f	76	v
27	'	37	7	47	G	57	W	67	g	77	w
28	(	38	8	48	H	58	X	68	h	78	x
29	)	39	9	49	I	59	Y	69	i	79	y
2A	*	3A	:	4A	J	5A	Z	6A	j	7A	z
2B	+	3B	;	4B	K	5B	[	6B	k	7B	{
2C	,	3C	<	4C	L	5C	\	6C	l	7C	|
2D	-	3D	=	4D	M	5D	]	6D	m	7D	}
2E	.	3E	>	4E	N	5E	^	6E	n	7E	~
2F	/	3F	?	4F	O	5F	_	6F	o	7F	¬

D.3   DECIMAL AND HEXADECIMAL CONVERSION

In Chapter 1 the use of hexadecimal notation was introduced. This is common in computing, as it permits the expression of a standard 16 bit word in only four characters and gives direct conversion to binary. For example:

1100 0101 1001 0110 = C596 and 0100 1000 0011 1111 = 483F

To convert hexadecimal to decimal and vice versa, two simple rules are used, with the table below.

HEX (100,000) DEC	HEX 10,000 DEC	HEX 1,000 DEC	HEX 100 DEC	HEX 10 DEC	HEX 1 DEC
0 0	0 0	0 0	0 0	0 0	0 0
1 1,048,576	1 65,536	1 4,096	1 256	1 16	1 1
2 2,097,152	2 131,072	2 8,192	2 512	2 32	2 2
3 3,145,728	3 196,608	3 12,288	3 768	3 48	3 3
4 4,194,304	4 262,144	4 16,384	4 1,024	4 64	4 4
5 5,242,880	5 327,680	5 20,480	5 1,280	5 80	5 5
6 6,291,456	6 393,216	6 24,576	6 1,536	6 96	6 6
7 7,340,032	7 458,752	7 28,672	7 1,792	7 112	7 7
8 8,388,608	8 524,288	8 32,768	8 2,048	8 128	8 8
9 9,437,184	9 589,824	9 36,864	9 2,304	9 144	9 9
A 10,485,760	A 655,360	A 40,960	A 2,560	A 160	A 10
B 11,534,336	B 720,896	B 45,056	B 2,816	B 176	B 11
C 12,582,912	C 786,432	C 49,152	C 3,072	C 192	C 12
D 13,631,488	D 851,968	D 53,248	D 3,328	D 208	D 13
E 14,680,064	E 917,504	E 57,344	E 3,584	E 224	E 14
F 15,728,640	F 983,040	F 61,440	F 3,840	F 240	F 15

To convert HEXADECIMAL to DECIMAL, find each hex digit in the column it corresponds to and note the decimal equivalent. Adding all the decimal parts gives the decimal equivalent of the original hexadecimal number.

To convert DECIMAL to HEXADECIMAL, find the largest decimal value in the table which will subtract from your number, do so and get the remainder. Note the hex equivalent of the value in its correct column. Take the remainder and repeat the process, and repeat it for all subsequent remainders. The answer is given by the hex values noted, with zero put in any blank column.

D.4 HEXADECIMAL ARITHMETIC, ADDITION AND MULTIPLICATION

As hexadecimal and binary arithmetic may not be obvious to the reader, tables are provided showing the results of simple addition and multiplication in hexadecimal. These can be directly compared with the binary form of course.

ADDITION

	1	2	3	4	5	6	7	8	9	A	B	C	D	E	F
1	02	03	04	05	06	07	08	09	0A	0B	0C	0D	0E	0F	10
2	03	04	05	06	07	08	09	0A	0B	0C	0D	0E	0F	10	11
3	04	05	06	07	08	09	0A	0B	0C	0D	0E	0F	10	11	12
4	05	06	07	08	09	0A	0B	0C	0D	0E	0F	10	11	12	13
5	06	07	08	09	0A	0B	0C	0D	0E	0F	10	11	12	13	14
6	07	08	09	0A	0B	0C	0D	0E	0F	10	11	12	13	14	15
7	08	09	0A	0B	0C	0D	0E	0F	10	11	12	13	14	15	16
8	09	0A	0B	0C	0D	0E	0F	10	11	12	13	14	15	16	17
9	0A	0B	0C	0D	0E	0F	10	11	12	13	14	15	16	17	18
A	0B	0C	0D	0E	0F	10	11	12	13	14	15	16	17	18	19
B	0C	0D	0E	0F	10	11	12	13	14	15	16	17	18	19	1A
C	0D	0E	0F	10	11	12	13	14	15	16	17	18	19	1A	1B
D	0E	0F	10	11	12	13	14	15	16	17	18	19	1A	1B	1C
E	0F	10	11	12	13	14	15	16	17	18	19	1A	1B	1C	1D
F	10	11	12	13	14	15	16	17	18	19	1A	1B	1C	1D	1E

MULTIPLICATION

	1	2	3	4	5	6	7	8	9	A	B	C	D	E	F
1															
2		04	06	08	0A	0C	0E	10	12	14	16	18	1A	1C	1E
3		06	09	0C	0F	12	15	18	1B	1E	21	24	27	2A	2D
4		08	0C	10	14	18	1C	20	24	28	2C	30	34	38	3C
5		0A	0F	14	19	1E	23	28	2D	32	37	3C	41	46	4B
6		0C	12	18	1E	24	2A	30	36	3C	42	48	4E	54	5A
7		0E	15	1C	23	2A	31	38	3F	46	4D	54	5B	62	69
8		10	18	20	28	30	38	40	48	50	58	60	68	70	78
9		12	1B	24	2D	36	3F	48	51	5A	63	6C	75	7E	87
A		14	1E	28	32	3C	46	50	5A	64	6E	78	82	8C	96
B		16	21	2C	37	42	4D	58	63	6E	79	84	8F	9A	A5
C		18	24	30	3C	48	54	60	6C	78	84	90	9C	A8	B4
D		1A	27	34	41	4E	5B	68	75	82	8F	9C	A9	B6	C3
E		1C	2A	38	46	54	62	70	7E	8C	9A	A8	B6	C4	D2
F		1E	2D	3C	4B	5A	69	78	87	96	A5	B4	C3	D2	E1

Index